T0277649

Let's Bake!

Over 100 Dessert Recipes
for Gifting & Giving

Gail Sweeney

Hatherleigh Press is committed to preserving and
protecting the natural resources of the earth.
Environmentally responsible and sustainable practices
are embraced within the company's mission statement.

Visit us at www.hatherleighpress.com.

Let's Bake

Cover and Interior Design by Carolyn Kasper
Photography by Gail Sweeney & Michael Sweeney, CSC

Printed in the United States
10 9 8 7 6 5 4 3 2 1

I would like to dedicate this book to all the bakers, cooks, and chefs out there who work very long (often unpaid) hours to perfect their craft, but whose greatest pleasure comes from knowing they have made someone happy with their food.

To my children, Madeleine, Carlin, Margot and to my grandson and sous baker, Elliot, may you always share your sweet side.

Contents

The Gift of Giving vii

Reading the Recipes ix

THE RECIPES

Cookies · 3

Brownies & Bars · 79

Cakes · 99

Tarts, Pies & Pastries · 163

Desserts for a Crowd · 221

**Simple Accompaniments to
Make Your Desserts Pop · 245**

About the Author 254

Recipe Index. 255

The Gift of Giving

I HAVE BEEN BAKING PASSIONATELY for the better part of 25 years, supplying specialty markets, boutique stores, bistros and (of course) my friends and family with my sweets. Late one night in my kitchen, as I was experimenting with new flavor combinations, I realized that the most satisfaction I get from my baking comes from the happiness it brings to others. It is amazing to me how the sharing of a plate of fresh baked cookies or the unveiling of a special vanilla layer cake can bring people together.

To this day, I remember making caramel filled chocolate cookies for the first time and presenting them to a group of work friends during a coffee break. Their eyes lit up, the word got out, and soon the whole office was crowded around this one small table. I met people who had been in the building for years for the very first time. Laughing and chatting, I also asked for their opinions on whether or not to leave the cookie as is or add more chocolate. But the important thing is that this was a memorable occasion for both me and them. What started as a tradition of sharing treats every Friday afternoon—sometimes with my colleagues serving as my taste testers—more often than not became a joyous occasion of celebrating the moment.

Sharing and gifting special desserts has been a lifelong joy for me. I feel very fortunate to have been able to make life a little more enjoyable at times for all those wonderful people who became an integral part of my baking experience, connecting with me and each other through the sharing of homemade food.

I began writing this baking book during the long months of COVID-19. I was baking feverishly for weeks on end and had more sweets in my kitchen than my family could possibly eat. Through social media and word of mouth, I made it known that desserts would be put out onto a bench in the parkette across from where I was living, at a certain time each day. If you build it, they will come—and several people did just that. My desserts were taken by a variety of people.

But the most surprising part of this story is that almost everyone left something in the dessert's place: a gadget to check the air in your tires; a pen; a bottle opener; all sorts of items were found in the space which once was occupied by a bag of chocolate chip cookies or a cake. I came to appreciate that when you engage in small acts of kindness it has an exponential effect on others, who in turn want to pay it forward. I keep these gifts in a special place in my house and in my heart.

For me, this baking book is all about those years I have spent creating beautiful desserts to be shared by a community of others: friends, family, neighbors, colleagues, and one-time strangers.

I hope that my readers will be able to share these recipes with friends and family and through their acts of giving create even stronger bonds amongst their loved ones, making the world a sweeter place.

Reading the Recipes

THIS BOOK IS ABOUT the pleasure of giving and sharing food with others. All the recipes in this book have evolved from baking for others for everyday occasions such as work coffee breaks and family outings, to school fundraisers, special event holidays and more festive celebrations such as engagement parties, birthdays and weddings. The sharing of food from one kitchen to another creates a special bond between people. Making homemade treats to give to others may seem like a small gesture but it conveys the important message that you value them which evokes a feeling of togetherness among people which in turn contributes to some of life's more special moments.

In this book, I have chosen recipes that gift well. They can be made ahead, keep well in the freezer, travel well and look pretty in a box or on a platter. Most of my recipes are made for sharing and they can be doubled to feed any size of crowd. They also can be halved to provide for smaller groups.

INGREDIENTS & SUBSTITUTIONS
Butter

I always use salted, rather than sweet or unsalted butter, unless otherwise specified. A good quality salted butter is not only less expensive but can last for a very long time on the counter, or in the refrigerator. Most of my recipes call for salted butter at room temperature.

Chocolate Callets

When you read chocolate callets it refers to Callebaut Belgian callets, which are slightly bigger and have a rounder shape than Chipits. Sometimes callets are referred to as wafers. Other brands, besides Callebaut, do make callets. Cacao Barry has very good callets, for example. However, you can conveniently buy Callebaut callets at Bulk Barn, Costco and Whole Foods or you can order them online from Amazon. Many of my recipes call for Callebaut dark chocolate callets which consist of approximately 54% cocoa. Sometimes this cocoa content is referred to as semi-sweet. Milk chocolate callets consist of approximately 34% cocoa content. You can substitute Chipits for callets, but the taste and texture suffers.

Chopped Chocolate

Anywhere that callets or Chipits are called for, you can substitute any good quality chopped chocolate bar. If I am substituting chopped chocolate for dark chocolate callets, I usually use a good quality 70% cocoa bar, such as Lindt or Green & Black. The percentage on a chocolate bar tells you how much of the bar, by weight, is made from the actual cacao bean. In cookies, adding chopped chocolate tends to add a lovely, layered quality to the texture of the cookie.

Flour

When you read flour, it refers to all-purpose flour unless otherwise specified. Flours vary in gluten levels with more gluten adding more structure. Cake flour, for example, has a lower gluten content and often is used in making white cakes or roulades, which have a finer crumb. Whole wheat flour also has less gluten than all-purpose flour and adds more nutritional value, in addition to a nutty flavor to baked goods. Bread flour has the most gluten, which is useful for promoting the more dense structure of most breads.

Eggs

Recipes almost always call for large eggs at room temperature, which makes for easier blending and better volume.

Sugar

When you read sugar it refers to fine white sugar as opposed to superfine, fruit, or castor sugar. Superfine, fruit and castor sugars are simply white sugar that has been very finely ground. When you read brown sugar, it refers to dark brown sugar, which contains more molasses.

When you read icing sugar this is the same as powdered or confectioners sugar, usually used to make icings or frostings.

COMMON SUBSTITUTIONS

When the recipe calls for buttermilk: If you do not have buttermilk, place 1 tablespoon of lemon juice in 1 cup of regular 2% milk.

When the recipe calls for superfine, castor or fruit sugar: Simply pulse regular white sugar in a food processor for 1 or 2 minutes.

When the recipe calls for cake flour: For 1 cup of cake flour measure out ¾ cup all-purpose flour plus 2 tablespoons of cornstarch.

When the recipe calls for sour cream: 1 cup plain yogurt = 1 cup sour cream

A FEW HELPFUL BAKING TIPS
Mixing Dry Ingredients

I dislike cleaning up, especially from my experimental bakes, when I have wildly added flavors and ingredients and tossed multiple mixing bowls into the kitchen sink. To save a bowl, I hand whisk my dry ingredients together on a piece of parchment paper. It saves sifting the flour and it is so much easier to tip into the bowl of the stand mixer. However, I still sift cake flour, icing sugar and cocoa powder.

Bringing Eggs to Room Temperature

Place fridge cold eggs in a bowl and run hot water over them. Let them sit in the hot water for a few minutes.

Beating Egg Whites & Egg Yolks Separately

Recipes for flourless cakes, roulades and mousses often call for beating egg yolks and egg whites, separately, at the beginning and end of the recipe, respectively. I always beat the egg whites first in the bowl of my stand mixer. I then empty the beaten egg whites into a fresh mixing bowl. With a quick wipe of the bowl and whisk, I move on to whisking the egg yolks. This saves getting out a handheld electric mixer to beat the whites at the end of the recipe, which is not only space consuming but requires more clean up (something which I try to limit at all times).

Rolling Out Dough

I always roll out pastry and cookie dough between sheets of waxed paper. It saves on clean-up, prevents sticking and makes the job of rolling out the dough much more fun.

Food Processor Pastry Crust

The one thing I have learned about pastry crust, and it took a *really* long time, is **not to overwork** the dough, and that is why I use a food processor. It is fast and does not transfer heat to the butter. Stop the food processor early. Do not wait until the dough comes together in a ball. Pulse a few times to incorporate the butter, then dump the ragged dough out onto a piece of floured parchment paper or into a large mixing bowl. Bring the dough together with floured hands and/or the help of the parchment paper.

Preventing Soggy Bottom Pastry

When working with cookie crumb crusts, I often add ½ cup of chopped chocolate to the crumbs and/or ½ cup of a nut flour. This not only adds another dimension of flavor to the crust, but helps to prevent the crust from becoming soggy, over time. When working with flour crusts for fruit pies or tarts, I toss a couple of tablespoons of nut flour (usually almond) over the pre-baked or blind-baked shell. The nut flour helps sop up the extra juices from the baking fruits. When working with custard-based tarts or pies, I brush the bottom of the blind-baked or fully baked pie shell with a beaten egg white. The egg white serves as a barrier to the custard fillings.

Blind Baking the Crust

I have included instructions on how to partially and fully blind-bake a crust in the recipes for A Lemon Tart Worth Sharing (page 164) and Coconut Cream Pie (page 199), respectively. I don't think I ever have **not** blind-baked a flour-based pie crust. It seems difficult at first, but once you have the pie weights (I use beans) and the technique of crumpling up a piece of parchment paper, placing it over the uncooked crust, and filling it with the weights, it saves so much heartache. There is nothing worse than looking at a picture-perfect pie, only to realize the pastry underneath still is raw.

Frosting Cakes

Place the cake layers in the freezer or refrigerator for 30 minutes, before frosting. This allows you to frost the cake without applying a crumb coat first. A crumb coat is a thin layer of icing that you apply to the tops and sides of the cake, before you actually put the final layer of buttercream on the cake. It gets rid of the small crumbs, which can affect the look of the finished product. However, I have found that I can avoid this step if I get the cake layers very cold, before I frost.

Freezing Cakes, Pies & Tarts

Always freeze cakes and pies on a parchment lined cookie sheet, unwrapped. As soon as they are frozen, wrap in plastic wrap with a covering of aluminum foil. Thaw in the original packaging in the refrigerator or remove the packaging and let stand at room temperature, uncovered.

Stabilizing Whipped Cream

This is a bakery trick to keep desserts looking and tasting as good as the day they were made. If you want to serve a dessert made with whipped cream hours after it is made, stabilize the whipped cream by adding 3 tablespoons of skim milk powder to 1 cup of whipping cream, before whipping. A more complicated method is adding gelatin, but the cream has a much longer lasting shelf life. I have used the gelatin method for making whipped cream in the recipes for Mille Feuille (page 216) and Light as Air Angel Food Cake (page 155).

TOOLS YOU CAN USE
Stand Mixer

The purchase of my stand mixer, only 10 years ago, changed my baking life. Not only can you easily double recipes, but it is very hard to over whip cream and egg whites, when you use a stand mixer with a whisk attachment. Not to mention that you can send texts and answer work phone calls as the stand mixer brings the cream and/or egg whites to the correct consistency.

Digital Instant Read Food Thermometer

While I often eyeball a simple caramel syrup, when it really counts, I always use my digital instant read thermometer. There is much work and expense involved in making Macarons or Italian buttercream and you just can't afford the time and money to make a mistake by having your temperature off by a few degrees.

Weight Scale

Most of the dry and wet ingredients in the following recipes have been weighed in grams and/or ounces on a good weight scale and then have been converted to cups. Nowadays good weight scales are not expensive and are available in most hardware stores. It is a very convenient way to work with all kinds of recipes, which may use grams or ounces, depending on where they originate.

Offset Spatulas

Have a good supply of offset spatulas in all sizes. I mainly use the smaller ones. They are good for smoothing out cake batter in the pan, frosting all kinds of confections, lifting finicky decorations, releasing tarts, and catching dripping chocolate from cookies. The larger ones can help you plate cakes. I have at least six!

Simple But Elegant Presentations

By no means am I a fine artist and my decorations tend to be simple and organic in nature. I rarely use fondant, gum paste or sprinkles. I try to stay away from regular food coloring, using plant based colored gels occasionally and very moderately. I find the nicest presentations often are the simplest: garnishes of fresh fruit, a chocolate drizzle, chopped pralines or edible flowers all provide a beautiful enhancement to a baked good.

THE
RECIPES

Cookies

Anzac Cookies For The 20 'Ohs

Preparation Time: 20 minutes / **Baking Time:** 15 to 18 minutes.

Equipment: *Three 12 x 18-inch parchment lined baking sheets, a large bowl and a medium or large cookie scoop.*

Anzac cookies historically became popular in Australia and New Zealand as part of the World War 1 fundraising effort. At this time, they were a much drier, more plain biscuit than this version, which contains more butter and additional ground spices such as nutmeg and cinnamon for a flavor boost. This is a one bowl recipe, which is fabulous for cleaning up and making with the family. With its mixture of oats, honey, and bran flakes, you can feel good about eating them all day and even sharing them with your kids. These cookies make great gifts for those who are health conscious.

2 cups toasted large flaked quick oats divided (½ cup for garnish)

1 cup bran flakes (lightly crushed by hand)

1 cup raisins

1½ cups flour

½ teaspoon salt

¼ teaspoon nutmeg

½ teaspoon cinnamon

½ cup white sugar

½ cup packed brown sugar

1 cup butter

3 heaping tablespoons honey

2 tablespoons water

1 heaping teaspoon of baking soda

Finely grated zest of 1 orange

Preheat the oven to 350°F. Evenly distribute the oats on a lined cookie sheet and bake for 8 minutes until fragrant and browned. Set aside. Reserve ½ cup of the warm oats for garnish and sprinkle them with sea salt. Combine the rest of the oats, bran, flour, salt, both sugars, raisins, nutmeg, cinnamon, and orange zest in a large bowl and set aside.

Heat the butter, honey, and water in a small saucepan over low to medium heat, stirring occasionally, until the butter melts. Remove the saucepan from the heat and quickly stir in the baking soda, stirring until the mixture becomes frothy. Make a well in the center of the dry ingredients. Pour the wet ingredients into the well and mix thoroughly. Using a medium to large size cookie scoop, scoop the dough into balls. Place the cookies on the prepared baking sheets about 2 inches apart.

Bake for 15 to 18 minutes until the cookies are golden brown. Take a look after 12 minutes as, due to the honey, these cookies can easily burn. Sprinkle the warm cookies with the toasted salted oats, while they are still on the sheets. Allow the cookies to cool for 5 minutes before transferring them to a wire rack to cool, completely. These cookies can be kept in airtight containers in the refrigerator for 1 week or can be frozen for up to 1 month.

ANZAC stands for Australian and New Zealand Army Corps. Anzac Day is April 25 and it marks the first major military action (Gallipoli) fought by the Anzac forces during WWI.

Overnight Rich & Gooey Chocolate Chip Cookies

Preparation Time: 20 minutes / **Chilling Time:** Overnight / **Baking Time:** 15 minutes

Equipment: *Three 12 x 18-inch parchment lined cookie sheets, a stand mixer fitted with the paddle attachment or handheld mixer, a large mixing bowl for storing the dough overnight in the refrigerator.*

I once was asked to make eighty Christmas gift boxes of cookies for a law firm by a friend, who suddenly found herself without her usual supplier for the firm's client gifts. I had two weeks to prepare over 1,000 cookies. I ended up filling gorgeous hat boxes with this chocolate chip cookie recipe. The clients' feedback was over the moon.

3½ cups flour

1¼ teaspoons baking soda

1½ teaspoons baking powder

½ teaspoon salt

1¼ cups room temperature butter

1 cup dark brown sugar

1 cup white sugar

2 large eggs at room temperature

2 teaspoons pure vanilla extract

2 cups dark or milk chocolate Callebaut callets or Chipits

1¼ cups good quality chopped dark chocolate (two 100-gram 70% chocolate bars)

Coarse sea salt for sprinkling on the warm cookies

Whisk all the dry ingredients together on a large piece of parchment paper. In the bowl of a stand mixer, cream together the butter and the two sugars. Add the eggs one at a time, beating well after each addition. Scrape down the sides of the bowl, when needed. Add the vanilla. With the mixer on low speed, tip the dry ingredients into the butter mixture until just combined. Fold in the chocolate.

Remove the dough to a large mixing bowl and cover with plastic wrap. Refrigerate for 12 hours or overnight. Note: Alternatively, you can shape the dough into four logs and freeze. When ready to bake, thaw at room temperature for 20 minutes, cut the logs into ⅓ inch slices and bake at 365°F for 15 minutes.

Take the bowl of cookie dough out of the refrigerator 30 minutes before you plan to bake the cookies.

Preheat the oven to 365°F. With a medium size cookie scoop, generously scoop out rounded balls of dough. Place the dough on the baking sheets, 2 inches apart. Bake for approximately 15

minutes until the cookies are golden brown, but the centers still look somewhat soft. Remove from the oven and sprinkle the warm cookies with coarse sea salt. Let cool completely on wire racks. These cookies can be refrigerated in airtight containers for up to 2 weeks or frozen for up to 3 months.

White Chocolate Pecan Cookies

Preparation Time: 15 minutes / **Chilling Time:** 30 minutes / **Baking Time:** 15 minutes

Equipment: *A stand mixer fitted with the paddle attachment or a handheld mixer, four 12 x 18-inch cookie sheets lined with parchment paper, a medium cookie scoop.*

I am always delightfully surprised at just how delicious the combination of white chocolate and toasted pecans is in a baked good. It really is a dynamite duo. I often serve these cookies warm with ice cream for dessert at dinner parties. I just freeze the balls of dough on a baking sheet the day before the party and bake them for 20 minutes straight out of the freezer as the guests are finishing up their main course. It never ceases to impress them!

1 cup butter at room temperature

1 cup packed brown sugar

½ cup white sugar

2 eggs at room temperature

2 cups Callebaut white chocolate callets or good quality chopped white chocolate bars (I used three 100-gram Lindt white chocolate bars)

1 cup toasted pecans

2 teaspoons vanilla

½ teaspoon salt

3 cups flour

1 teaspoon baking soda

Toast the pecans at 350°F for 7 minutes. Whisk together the flour, salt, and baking soda on a large sheet of parchment paper.

In the bowl of the stand mixer, cream the butter and the two sugars until light and fluffy.

Add the eggs one at a time, mixing on medium high speed after each addition. Tip the flour into the butter mixture and mix until just incorporated.

On low speed, add the chocolate and chopped toasted pecans, until evenly distributed. Using a medium size scoop, generously scoop the dough out onto the prepared baking sheets, about 2½ inches apart.

Chill the sheets of dough in the refrigerator for approximately 30 minutes.

Preheat the oven to 365°F. Bake the cookies for approximately 12 to 15 minutes, until just set and golden brown. Let the cookies cool on the sheets. These cookies can be stored in airtight containers in the refrigerator for 5 days or in the freezer for 2 months.

Oatmeal Raisin Coconut Chocolate Chip Cookies

Preparation Time: 20 minutes / **Chilling Time:** 1 hour / **Baking Time:** 15 minutes

Equipment: *Three 12 x 18-inch cookie sheets, a stand mixer fitted with the paddle attachment, or handheld mixer, medium to large cookie scoop.*

I call these cookies my picnic cookies because, whenever we decide to picnic at the beach or in a park, we take these chocked full of goodness cookies with us. They are not too sweet but deliciously satisfying to savor after a swim or a hike. Later in the book, I describe how I sweeten and toast organic coconut for both the Coconut Cake and Coconut Pie. I go through the same process for these cookies, which results in a crunchy not too sweet coconut addition, lending the cookie a natural sweetness and lovely crisp texture. For ease of baking, I will include the coconut sweetening instructions again, here.

1½ cups flour

2 cups large flaked quick oats

1 teaspoon baking soda

½ teaspoon salt

1 cup brown sugar

½ cup white sugar

1 cup butter

2 large eggs at room temperature

1¼ cups unsweetened organic coconut, sweetened and toasted (recipe follows)

1 cup raisins

2 cups dark (54%) or milk chocolate Callebaut callets or Chipits

COOKIES

On a large piece of parchment paper, whisk together the flour, oats, baking soda and salt.

In the bowl of the stand mixer, cream the butter. Add both sugars and mix until light and fluffy. Add the eggs one at a time, beating after each addition. Tip in the dry ingredients and mix until just combined. On low speed, add the raisins, coconut, and chocolate chips until blended. Scrape down to the bottom of the bowl with a spatula to make sure all the ingredients are evenly distributed throughout the dough.

Scoop out medium sized balls of dough and place them 2 inches apart on the prepared baking sheets. Place the sheets in the refrigerator for 30 minutes or longer until the dough is cold.

Preheat the oven to 365°F. Bake the cookies for 15 minutes and let cool on racks or on the sheets. These cookies can be kept for 7 days in the refrigerator or can be frozen up to 1 month in airtight containers.

SWEETENING & TOASTING THE COCONUT

Preheat the oven to 350°F. In a medium saucepan combine ½ cup water, ½ cup sugar, and 2 teaspoons of vanilla. Heat until all the sugar is dissolved. Add the coconut and stir until the coconut is evenly coated with syrup. Remove the coconut with a slotted spoon or spatula and spread out on a parchment lined baking sheet. Bake until the edges of the coconut become golden brown, about 7 minutes, stirring halfway through so that the coconut browns, evenly. Set aside to cool. If you like a fine coconut and the coconut is in larger pieces you can give it a finer chop.

Empty Drawer Cookies

Preparation Time: 15 to 20 minutes / **Chilling Time:** 30 minutes / **Baking Time:** 15 minutes

Equipment: Equipment: *A stand mixer fitted with the paddle attachment or handheld mixer, four 12 x 18-inch parchment lined baking sheets, a large size cookie scoop.*

Empty Drawer cookies are a tribute to Hedy Goldsmith, who began her career as a pastry chef in 1990, working in Florida and California. Her principle was to make simple, crave worthy desserts, filled with childhood memories. Hedy served her cookies containing pretzels and potato chips, among other things, warm in her LA restaurants. Feel free to go crazy with this recipe. You can add anything you want to these cookies as long as you have enough dough to hold the ingredients together. I have not added any nuts to these cookies making them perfect for fundraisers and school events.

1 cup butter at room temperature

1 cup packed brown sugar

½ cup white sugar

2 eggs at room temperature

3 cups flour

½ teaspoon salt

1¼ teaspoons baking soda

1½ teaspoons pure vanilla extract

1½ cups Callebaut milk chocolate callets or Chipits

1 cup Callebaut dark (54%) callets or Chipits

2 cups crinkle potato chips

½ cup malted milk balls cut in half

2 Skor bars chopped roughly into ¼ inch pieces

1 cup Smarties or M&Ms, divided (¾ cup for the recipe, ¼ cup reserved for decorating the tops of the cookies)

Chop up the Skor bars into ¼ inch pieces, dust very lightly with flour and place in the freezer. Place 2 cups of potato chips into a closed plastic bag and crush with a rolling pin, or with your hand, into small coarse pieces.

Whisk the flour, baking soda and salt together on a large piece of parchment paper.

Add the butter and both sugars to the stand mixer and beat on medium high speed till light and creamy. Add the eggs one at a time, beating well after each addition. Add the vanilla.

With the mixer on low, tip the dry ingredients into the mixer and mix until the flour is incorporated. Bring the Skor bar pieces out of the freezer. Start adding the treats to your cookie dough beginning with the chocolate callets or Chipits, Smarties, malted milk balls, Skor bar pieces. Add the chips at the end so they do not become potato flour in your dough. Mix until just incorporated.

With a medium or large size cookie scoop, scoop out the dough onto your lined sheets, about 2 inches apart. Chill cookies on the sheets in the refrigerator for 30 minutes.

Preheat oven to 350°F. Bake for 15 to 20 minutes until browned around the edges, but still a little soft in the center. Decorate the tops of the cookies with the leftover Smarties or M&Ms. Let cool on sheets. Cookies can be refrigerated for 2 weeks in airtight containers or frozen for up to 2 months.

Empty drawer cookies are nut free and perfect for fundraisers and school events.

Ginger Crinkle Cookies

Preparation Time: 20 minutes / **Chilling Time:** 1 hour / **Baking Time:** 12 minutes

---

Equipment: *Three 12 x 18-inch baking sheets, a stand mixer fitted with the paddle attachment or a handheld mixer, medium cookie scoop.*

This cookie has a pleasing texture and a perfect amount of spice for ginger lovers. Crisp on the outside, yet soft and chewy on the inside, you could not ask for a better crumb. The cookies are easily made; however, you do have to chill the dough balls on the baking sheets for 1 hour or the cookies will become flat in the oven and lose their crinkles. I love bringing these cookies as hostess gifts, in all kinds of pantry jars, during the holiday season.

2½ cups flour

2¾ teaspoons ground ginger

1¼ teaspoons baking soda

½ teaspoon salt

3 tablespoons finely chopped crystallized ginger

1 cup butter at room temperature

1¼ cups white sugar

1 egg at room temperature

¼ cup molasses

½ cup white or fine raw brown sugar for coating the cookie balls (I use Plantation Raw Sugar)

Whisk together the flour, salt, baking soda, ginger powder and finely chopped crystallized ginger on a large piece of parchment paper.

In the bowl of the stand mixer, cream the butter with the sugar until light and fluffy. Add in the egg and beat on medium high speed until fully incorporated. Lower the speed, and stream in the molasses, continuing to mix until well blended. Tip in the dry ingredients and mix until just incorporated.

Pour raw brown sugar into a small bowl. With a small or medium cookie scoop, scoop out balls of dough, rolling each ball of dough in the sugar, before placing the balls on the prepared baking sheets, 2 inches apart. Refrigerate the balls of dough for 1 hour, before baking.

Preheat the oven to 360°F. Bake for 12 minutes until the cookies are lightly browned. Let cool on the sheets. The ginger flavor in the cookies will intensify over time. It is best to let the ginger flavor develop for at least 1 day, at room temperature, or in the refrigerator, before placing them in the freezer. Ginger is a natural preservative and consequently these cookies can be kept for over two weeks on the shelf or in the refrigerator and can be frozen for up to 3 months.

Pecan Snowball Cookies

Preparation Time: 20 minutes / **Chilling Time:** 1 hour / **Baking Time:** 15 to 20 minutes

Equipment: *Two 12 x 18-inch baking sheets, a stand mixer fitted with the paddle attachment, or handheld mixer, a food processor for grinding the nuts (optional).*

Sometimes called Mexican Wedding cookies, these little gems should be called Melt Aways as they are so delicate in texture. They traditionally are made with ground nuts, and you can use pecans, as I did here, or pistachios or hazelnuts. These cookies make lovely gifts and, of course, are perfect to package as wedding favors.

1 cup butter at room
   temperature

¾ cup icing sugar, sifted

1 cup finely chopped pecans,
   toasted

1¾ cups flour

½ teaspoon salt

2 teaspoons vanilla extract

1½ cups icing sugar for rolling
   the cookies

Preheat the oven to 350°F. Place the pecans on a baking sheet and toast for approximately 7 minutes until darkened and fragrant. When cool, place in the bowl of a food processor and pulse in short bursts until the nuts are finely chopped, but not powder. If you do not have a food processor, finely chop the nuts with a sharp knife.

On a large piece of parchment paper, whisk together the flour, nuts, and salt.

In the bowl of the stand mixer, cream the butter and sugar until light and fluffy, a good two or three minutes. Add the vanilla extract. Tip in the dry ingredients and mix until just incorporated.

Place 1½ cups of icing sugar into a bowl. With a small cookie scoop, scoop out balls of dough and roll them in the icing sugar, before placing them on the prepared baking sheets. Chill the cookies in the refrigerator for at least 1 hour, before baking.

Preheat the oven to 350°F. Bake the cookies for about 15 minutes until they start to color very slightly on the top. While the cookies still are warm, roll them once more in the icing sugar. Let cool completely on wire racks.

These cookies will keep in an airtight container for one week in the refrigerator or cupboard and can be frozen for up to 2 months.

Brown Butter Caramel Cookies

Preparation Time: 20 minutes / **Chilling Time:** 30 minutes / **Baking Time:** 15 minutes

Equipment: *Three 12 x 18-inch baking sheets lined with parchment paper, a stand mixer fitted with the paddle attachment or handheld mixer, a medium size cookie scoop.*

A rich nutty caramel flavor is created in this cookie by the addition of browned butter and salted caramel Chipits to the batter. Brown butter generally adds a subtle nutty dimension to food and is often used for flavoring vegetable pasta dishes. In cookies, it deepens the caramel notes, without adding sweetness. I have added some dark chocolate to this cookie as it contrasts beautifully with the caramel. It is without a doubt my husband's favorite cookie.

1 cup butter, browned

1 egg plus 1 yolk at room temperature

2½ cups flour

½ teaspoon baking powder

¼ teaspoon baking soda

¼ teaspoon salt

1½ cups dark brown sugar

2 teaspoons pure vanilla extract

¾ cup salted caramel Chipits

Two 100-gram 70% chocolate bars such as Lindt, chopped

Sea salt for sprinkling on finished cookies

Place the butter in a small saucepan and cook over medium heat, swirling the pan occasionally. The butter will froth up and you will see brown particles forming along the top of the butter. Stir the butter occasionally and when the butter turns into a dark amber color, remove from the heat. Set aside to cool in the fridge and continue with the rest of the recipe.

Chop the chocolate bars into small ¼-inch size pieces. On a large piece of parchment paper, whisk together the flour, baking powder, baking soda and salt.

Place the cooled brown butter into the bowl of the stand mixer. There will be browned bits at the bottom of the pan and add these as well as they will intensify the flavor.

Add the brown sugar to the butter and mix on medium high speed until light and creamy.

Add the egg and yolk and continue beating until well incorporated. Tip in the dry ingredients and mix until just combined. On low speed, add in the caramel Chipits and chopped chocolate.

Scoop rounded balls of dough onto the prepared cookie sheets, 2 inches apart. Refrigerate for 30 minutes.

Preheat the oven to 360°F. Bake the cookies for approximately 15 minutes or until set and golden brown around the edges. Sprinkle the warm cookies with sea salt. Let cool on the trays. Cookies can be refrigerated in airtight containers for 1 week or can be frozen for up to 2 months.

These cookies will keep in an airtight container for one week in the refrigerator or cupboard and can be frozen for up to 2 months.

S'more Cookies

Preparation Time: 20 minutes / **Chilling Time:** 30 minutes / **Baking Time:** 12 minutes

Equipment: *Three 12 x 18-inch baking sheets, lined with parchment paper, a stand mixer fitted with the paddle attachment or handheld mixer.*

Who does not like a S'more cookie? It's not just the memory of childhood summer campfires, but the actual combination of ingredients, which is so tantalizing. This cookie is composed of graham cracker crumbs, chocolate, marshmallows, Skor bars, and Nutella. I would have added some bananas, but just could not figure out how to keep the cookies from going mushy after a day or two. This cookie is the one cookie that tastes so much better than any photo can convey.

1¼ cups graham cracker crumbs

2½ cups flour

½ teaspoon salt

¼ teaspoon baking soda

1 teaspoon baking powder

1 cup butter, room temperature

¾ cup brown sugar

¾ cup white sugar

2 eggs, room temperature

2 teaspoons vanilla

2 cups mini marshmallows plus ½ cup for garnish

3 Skor bars, chopped

2 cups milk chocolate Callebaut callets or Chipits or chopped chocolate

½ cup dark (54%) Callebaut callets or Chipits or chopped chocolate for garnish

½ cup Nutella

Chop up the Skor bars into ¼ inch pieces, lightly flour, and place them in the freezer.

On a large piece of parchment paper, whisk together the graham crumbs, flour, salt, baking soda and baking powder. In the bowl of the stand mixer, cream together the butter and both sugars until smooth. Add the eggs, one at a time, beating well after each addition, until the mixture is light and fluffy. Add the vanilla. Tip in the dry ingredients and mix until blended. Add the chocolate, Skor pieces and marshmallows. Take the bowl off the stand and add the Nutella to the dough in tablespoons, being careful to keep it separate enough so that you can see it in sections, rather than turning the dough into a uniform color. With a large cookie scoop, scoop out mounds of dough onto the prepared baking sheets, two inches apart. Chill the dough for 30 minutes.

Preheat the oven to 365°F. Bake the cookies for 12 to 15 minutes until browned around the edges but still a little soft in the center. Remove from the oven and place a few chocolate chips on each one, followed by 3 or 4 mini marshmallows. Place back in the oven just until the marshmallows reach a golden brown color. Let cool on the sheets for 10 minutes before removing to wire racks.

These cookies can be kept in airtight containers in the refrigerator for 4 days and can be frozen for up to 3 months. They are terrific warmed right out of the freezer in a 350°F oven for family and guests.

S'more cookies just say "summer!"

Ruby's Flourless Florentines

(GLUTEN-FREE)

Preparation Time: 15 minutes / **Baking Time:** 10 minutes

Equipment: *Three 12 x 18-inch parchment lined cookie sheets. 2 offset spatulas, a medium sized saucepan for making the cookies. A piping bag for decorating with melted chocolate.*

I love the nutty honeyed taste and crunch of Florentines. However, be prepared for some finicky work to keep these cookies in the flat rounded shape for which they are known. I use two small offset spatulas to flatten and shape the cookies when they begin to spread in the oven. Yes, I have burned my fingers more often than I can count, so be careful. To me, this fragrant almond buttery creation is worth the effort. I give them to my European friends who feel like they have just had a taste of home. Ruby is my Norwich terrier who managed to knock down a whole tray of cooling Florentines and eat at least 2 before I could stop her.

½ cup white sugar

½ cup butter cubed

2 heaping tablespoons of honey

¼ cup whipping cream

¼ teaspoon salt

2½ cups sliced almonds

1 tablespoon grated orange zest or zest of 1 large orange

½ cup chopped tart dried cherries

FINISHING CHOCOLATE

1 cup dark (54%) Callebaut chocolate callets or Chipits for drizzling on the finished cookies

Preheat the oven to 375°F.

Melt together the butter, sugar and honey in a medium large saucepan over medium heat. Increase the heat to high and allow the mixture to boil for approximately 3 minutes, stirring only occasionally. When the mixture reaches a rich amber color take the saucepan off the heat and add the cream and salt. It will boil up so be careful. Return the saucepan to the heat and allow to boil for 45 seconds. Take the saucepan off the heat again and add the almonds and dried cherries. Stir the mixture until the almond and cherries are evenly incorporated. Allow the cookies to cool for 5 minutes.

Drop 1 heaping tablespoon of the cookie mixture onto the baking sheets about 3 inches apart. These cookies will spread so make sure to leave enough room for them to expand. I make

6 per one 12 x 18-inch cookie sheet. Place only 1 cookie sheet in the oven at a time. You will have to tidy up the cookies as they begin to caramelize and spread, with an oiled offset spatula. Annoying as this may be, the finished result looks absolutely amazing. Bake for 10 minutes or until the Florentines are a rich golden brown. Cool the cookies completely on the baking sheets.

FINISHING CHOCOLATE

While the cookies are cooling, melt the chocolate in a heat proof bowl over a saucepan of simmering water, stirring frequently until the chocolate is melted and warm to the touch. Place the chocolate in a piping bag, or using a fork to drizzle, cover the tops of the cookies with chocolate stripes. Allow the chocolate to set at room temperature for 2 hours or in the refrigerator for 1 hour.

Store the Florentines between waxed paper in airtight containers. They will keep in the refrigerator for 5 days or can be frozen for up to 2 months.

Versatile & Delicious Sugar Cookies

Preparation Time: 15 minutes / **Chilling Time:** 2 hours / **Baking Time:** 15 minutes

Equipment: *Four 12 x 18-inch parchment lined cookie sheets, cookie cutters, a stand mixer fitted with the paddle attachment or handheld mixer, rolling pin, decorations of your choice.*

I have used this recipe for 20 years and it remains my grown-up children's favorite Christmas cookie. Whether sprinkled with raw sugar, sandwiched with raspberry jam, or covered with Royal icing and elegantly painted for special occasion gifts, these cookies are the first to go on the platter. This recipe makes a lot of cookies. However, you can cut the recipe in half, easily, and the cookies freeze beautifully. If you want to decorate with royal icing, you can buy premade royal icing at most bulk stores, but it is fairly easy to make, and I have included a no fail recipe for royal icing below.

COOKIES

2 cups salted butter at room
    temperature
1½ cups white sugar
2 large eggs at room
    temperature
1/4 teaspoon baking powder
½ teaspoon salt
2 teaspoons vanilla
4⅔ cups flour

NO FAIL ROYAL ICING

3 ounces pasteurized
   egg whites at room
   temperature (found in
   cartons in grocery stores)
1 teaspoon vanilla extract or
   ½ teaspoon lemon juice
4 cups icing sugar
Pinch of salt

COOKIES

Whisk together the flour, salt, and baking powder on a large sheet of parchment paper.

Place the butter and sugar in the bowl of the stand mixer and mix on medium speed until light and fluffy. Add the eggs one at a time, mixing well after each addition. Beat in the vanilla. With the mixer running on low, tip the flour mixture into the butter mixture, until the flour is just blended. Scrape the dough out onto a floured piece of parchment paper. Knead the dough a few times, using the paper to help you form the dough into a large smooth round. Divide the round of dough into 3 disks. Wrap the discs in plastic wrap and refrigerate for at least 2 hours or overnight.

Take the dough out of the refrigerator 20 minutes before you plan to roll it out.

Recipe continues on page 26

These cookies are so versatile that children can go wild on the holidays decorating them with all kinds of candy confections, or they can be hand painted for elegant gifts.

Place a disc of dough between two sheets of waxed paper and roll the dough out to ¼ inch thickness. Using any kind of cutter, cut the dough into shapes. Place the cookie shapes on the prepared cookie sheets 2 inches apart. To ensure the cookies keep their shape, place the sheets of cookies back in the refrigerator for 30 minutes. The sheets can be stacked one on top of the other with a piece of wax paper in between.

Preheat the oven to 350°F. Bake the cookies for approximately 15 minutes. While the cookies are still quite warm, you can brush them with a whisked pasteurized egg white, then decorate them with sprinkles or colored sugars. However, if you plan to finish the cookies with buttercream or royal icing, skip the egg white and cool the cookies completely. The cookies can be stored in airtight containers in the refrigerator for 1 week or in the freezer for 2 months.

ROYAL ICING

In the bowl of the stand mixer, fitted with the whisk attachment, whisk the egg whites until frothy. Add a pinch of salt. At low speed, gradually add the icing sugar and increase the speed once all the sugar has been incorporated. Continue beating on high speed until the mixture becomes glossy and is just beginning to form soft peaks. Add the vanilla extract or lemon juice and continue to beat until the extract is incorporated. If you find the mixture is too thick to pipe or spread onto the cookies easily, gradually add water, ½ teaspoon at a time. If you plan to use food coloring for decoration, divide the icing into separate bowls and mix in each color well. If not using the royal icing right away, cover the bowls with a damp, clean tea towel. Pipe or spoon the royal icing evenly onto each cookie and let set for at least 12 hours.

HAND PAINTING COOKIES

If you are planning to paint on the royal icing, the icing must be completely dry and it is best to leave the sheets of cookies out on a table in a dry place, overnight. To hand paint, mix a small amount of food coloring gel with a small amount of clear alcohol such as vodka. Just experiment with the amounts until you achieve a saturation of color that you like.

Cherry Almond Oat Rounds
in White Chocolate

Preparation Time: 30 minutes / **Chilling Time:** 30 minutes / **Baking Time:** 15 to 18 minutes

Equipment: *Three 12 x 18-inch parchment lined baking sheets, rolling pin, 1½ inch round cookie cutter, stand mixer fitted with the paddle attachment or hand-held mixer.*

This cookie with its combination of oats, dried cherries and almonds is not overly sweet, but has a knockout flavor combination. When topped with white chocolate, the cookie surprisingly maintains its subtlety, but tastes deliciously rich at the same time. I have added a touch of brandy to these cookies, however the brandy is optional.

¾ cup dried tart cherries

2 tablespoons orange juice

2 tablespoons brandy (optional)

1 cup sliced almonds, toasted

1 cup all-purpose flour

½ cup whole wheat flour

1½ cups large flaked quick oats

½ teaspoon salt

1 cup salted butter at room temperature

¾ cup white sugar

¼ teaspoon of freshly grated nutmeg
  or ¼ teaspoon of powdered nutmeg

¼ teaspoon of freshly grated cinnamon
  stick or ¼ teaspoon of powdered
  cinnamon

Finely grated zest of 1 large orange

WHITE CHOCOLATE FINISH

2 cups Callebaut white chocolate
  callets or Chipits or chopped
  white chocolate (you will need
  three 90 to 100-gram bars)

Place sliced almonds on a parchment lined baking sheet and toast in a preheated 350°F oven until browned and fragrant, about 7 minutes. Remove and let cool completely. Rough chop the almonds into smallish pieces. Cut up the dried cherries and place them in a drinking glass. Pour 2 tablespoons of orange juice and 2 tablespoons of brandy (if using) over the cherries. You can substitute the brandy with more orange juice. Microwave the cherries for 40 seconds.

Whisk together the oats, flours, salt, spices, and almonds on a large piece of parchment paper. In the bowl of a stand mixer fitted with the paddle attachment, cream the butter and sugar until light and fluffy. Add the orange zest. Tip in the dry ingredients and mix on low speed until just combined. Add the dried cherries, juice, and brandy (if using) and mix just until incorporated.

Scrape out the dough on a floured piece of parchment paper. With floured hands knead the dough a few times and roughly shape the dough into a large circle. Place a piece of wax paper over the dough and, with a rolling pin, finish rolling out the dough to a thickness of ¼ inch. Cut out rounds with a 1½ inch circle cookie cutter. Place the cookies 1½ inches apart on the prepared baking sheets. Chill the cookies for 30 minutes, before baking.

Preheat the oven to 350°F. Bake the cookies for 15 to 18 minutes or until golden brown. Let cool on racks.

FINISHING CHOCOLATE

Melt the white chocolate in a heatproof bowl over a saucepan of simmering water. There should be no more than 2 inches of water in the saucepan. Do not allow the chocolate to get too hot as white chocolate scorches easily. Dip the top of each cookie into the chocolate, removing any excess chocolate with an offset spatula.

Allow the chocolate to set at room temperature for 2 hours or in the refrigerator for 1 hour.

The cookies will keep in airtight containers for up to 2 weeks in the refrigerator or can be frozen for up to 2 months.

"Not Just A Cookie" Chocolate Dipped Espresso Hearts

Preparation Time: 15 minutes / **Chilling Time:** 1 hour / **Baking Time:** 20 to 25 minutes

Equipment: *Three 12 x 18 parchment lined baking sheets, stand mixer fitted with the paddle attachment or handheld mixer, a heart shaped cookie cutter.*

These espresso shortbreads became my signature cookie when I was catering and supplying boutique stores. One of my clients, when enjoying one of these cookies for the first time, looked up and said: "This is not just a cookie." We all laughed, and the name stuck to these delightful coffee shortbreads. The cookies are wonderful when enjoyed with a midday coffee or an after-dinner drink. I discovered that they also keep for an exceptionally long time in the refrigerator and much longer, up to 4 months, in the freezer. So rich in taste and lovely to look at, I began gifting these cookies for special occasions, such as Valentine's Day, finding inventive presentations such as small burlap coffee bags in which to place the cookies. Note: This recipe can easily be halved.

COOKIES

2 cups cold salted
   butter, cubed

1 cup white sugar

½ teaspoon salt

4 cups flour

4 tablespoons good quality
   finely ground espresso
   coffee

FINISHING CHOCOLATE

2 cups Callebaut dark (54%)
   chocolate callets or Chipits,
   or chopped chocolate
   (you will need four 100-
   gram dark chocolate bars,
   60 to 70%)

COOKIES

Whisk together the flour, salt, and espresso powder on a large sheet of parchment paper. Combine the cold butter with the sugar in the bowl of a stand mixer. On medium speed, mix until just combined, but not smooth. You still will see some rough pieces of butter. With the mixer on low speed, tip in the dry ingredients. When the dough just pulls together, stop mixing. It is important to not overmix at this stage.

Scrape the dough out of the mixer onto a floured piece of parchment paper. Knead the dough a few times before bringing the dough together in a ball. Shape the dough into 3 smooth round discs. Wrap the discs in plastic wrap and refrigerate the discs for 1 hour or longer.

Recipe continues on page 32

I branded these cookies *Not Just A Cookie* which also became my catering company's logo.

NOT JUST A COOKIE

Chocolate Dipped Espresso Cookies

Bring out the chilled dough 20 minutes before you plan to roll it. Roll between floured sheets of waxed paper to a ¼ inch thickness. Cut out the shapes (I use a medium size heart cutter) and place them on the baking sheets one inch apart. Chill the sheets of cookies for another 30 minutes to ensure a perfect shape, while baking. To save room in your fridge, you can stack the cookie sheets one on top of another with a piece of wax paper in between the sheets.

Preheat the oven to 325°F. Bake the cookies for 20 to 25 minutes.

FINISHING CHOCOLATE

Place the chocolate in a heat proof bowl over a saucepan of simmering water. The water in the pan should not be deeper than 2 inches. Stir the chocolate continuously, making sure the chocolate does not scorch. If you have a digital read thermometer, look for a temperature of approximately 32°C or 90°F. The chocolate should look glossy and feel quite warm to the touch, but not hot.

ASSEMBLY

Dip each cooled cookie (they can be made ahead and refrigerated) into the chocolate, coating only half the cookie. Scrape any excess chocolate off the sides of the cookie with an offset spatula. Place the dipped cookies on a cookie rack until the chocolate has firmed up (about 2 hours at room temperature or 1 hour in the refrigerator). Note: If while dipping the cookies the chocolate cools down and is getting less fluid, place the bowl back over the hot water, stirring until it reaches the right consistency. The cookies will keep in airtight containers in the refrigerator for 2 weeks and can be stored in the freezer for up to 4 months.

Almond Cherry Rectangles in White Chocolate

Preparation Time: 20 minutes / **Chilling Time:** 2 hours / **Baking Time:** 15 minutes

Equipment: *Three 12 x 18 parchment lined baking sheets, a stand mixer fitted with the paddle attachment or handheld mixer.*

This cookie makes for a delicious afternoon or evening treat with tea or coffee. The biscuits are not overly sweet, and the white chocolate complements the tart dried cherries perfectly. The toasted almonds lend a crunch and a nutty flavor to the biscuit, while the addition of lemon juice and zest heightens the overall flavor. The cookie dough is made into 4 rectangular logs, refrigerated, then sliced into cookies.

1½ cups butter at room temperature

1 cup sugar

1 tablespoon grated lemon rind

1 tablespoon lemon juice

1 tablespoon brandy (optional)

2 large egg yolks at room temperature

3 cups flour

½ teaspoon salt

1 cup toasted and chopped almonds

1 cup chopped dried cherries

FINISHING CHOCOLATE

2 cups white Callebaut chocolate callets or Chipits or chopped good quality white chocolate bars (you will need three 100-gram bars)

Mix together the sugar and lemon zest in a bowl. Set aside for 10 minutes.

Place the dried cherries in a drinking glass and pour the lemon juice and brandy, if using, over them. Microwave the cherries for 40 seconds. Bake the almonds in a 350°F oven for 5 to 7 minutes and rough chop them into smallish pieces. Set aside to cool.

Whisk together the flour and salt on a large piece of parchment paper. In the bowl of the stand mixer, cream together the butter and the sugar until light and fluffy. Add the yolks, one at a time, beating after each addition.

Stop the mixer and tip the flour into the bowl, then mix on low speed until the flour just is incorporated. Add the cherries and any remaining juice and brandy. Mix in the almonds.

Scrape the dough out onto a floured piece of parchment or wax paper. Knead the dough a few times, then divide the dough into four equal pieces. Form the dough into 4 rectangular logs,

Recipe continues on the next page

approximately 6 inches long, 1½ inches wide and 2 inches high. I use a bench scraper to coax the dough into a rectangular shape and bang each side of the rectangular logs on my counter to square off the sides. Wrap each of the logs in plastic wrap and refrigerate for at least 2 hours.

With a sharp knife, slice the logs into rectangular cookies, slightly thicker than ¼ inch. Place on the prepared cookie sheets 1½ inches apart. Refrigerate the cookie sheets for another 30 minutes. You can stack the trays one on top of another with a piece of wax paper in between.

Preheat the oven to 350°F. Bake for approximately 15 to 18 minutes until the cookies are lightly browned around the edges. Let the cookies cool on the sheets for at least 10 minutes before removing them to wire racks to cool completely.

FINISHING CHOCOLATE

Place the white chocolate in a heat proof bowl over a saucepan of simmering water. There should be no more than 2 inches of water in the bottom of the saucepan. White chocolate scorches easily, so stir constantly until melted and do not let the chocolate get too hot. If the chocolate seems to be heating up too quickly, simply take it off the burner and finish melting the chocolate off the heat.

ASSEMBLY

Dip the top of each cookie diagonally in the white chocolate, shake the cookie gently over the bowl and use an offset spatula to remove any drips. Let the chocolate set at room temperature for 2 hours or in the refrigerator for 1 hour.

These cookies can be stored in airtight containers in the refrigerator for 1 week or in the freezer for 3 months.

Holiday Thumbprint Cookies

Preparation Time: 20 minutes / **Chilling Time:** 1 hour / **Baking Time:** 25 minutes

Equipment: *Three 12 x 18-inch cookies sheets lined with parchment paper, a stand mixer fitted with the paddle attachment or handheld mixer, a small cookie scoop.*

Filled with one or two different types of jams or preserves, these cookies look particularly festive on a party platter. I usually use two jams of a contrasting color such as peach and blueberry. However, any combination of preserves or even just one jam works well here. These thumbprint cookies have a special added crunch to them because I dip the balls of dough into egg white and then into chopped almonds. I do not use my thumb to make the hole for the jam, rather I use the rounded end of my potato peeler. However, recently, when I was rushed off my feet for a Bistro cookie order, I got my husband to help me, and he used the bottle cap end of a beer bottle. It worked beautifully.

1 cup butter at room
    temperature

⅔ cup sugar

1 large egg yolk

1 teaspoon vanilla extract

2½ cups flour

½ teaspoon salt

1 cup of jam or preserves of
    your choice for filling the
    cookies

For Rolling Before Baking

2 egg whites, room
    temperature

¾ cup of toasted almonds,
    finely chopped

1 tablespoon of sugar

Lightly toast the almonds in a 350°F oven for 5 minutes. Give the almonds a fine chop and set aside in a bowl. When the almonds are cool, add one tablespoon of sugar and mix until combined.

Make the dough. In the bowl of the stand mixer, cream together the butter and sugar until light and fluffy. Add the egg yolk and vanilla. Whisk together the flour and salt on a piece of parchment paper and tip the flour into the butter mixture. Mix on low speed just until the flour has been incorporated.

Place the egg whites in a bowl and lightly whisk with a fork. Place the chopped almonds next to the bowl of egg whites.

With a small cookie scoop or tablespoon, form the dough into one-inch balls. Dip each ball into the egg white, then into the sugar/almond mixture. Place on the prepared cookie sheets, 1-inch apart. Make a deep indentation with your thumb or any rounded end of a kitchen tool in each cookie and place the cookies in the refrigerator to chill for 1 hour.

Preheat the oven to 350°F. Bake the unfilled cookies for 10 minutes. Remove from the oven and press down into the centers, once more. Warm the jam in the microwave for 35 seconds to loosen it. Fill each center with jam. Place the cookies back in the oven for another 12 minutes. Remove from the oven and let cool completely. These cookies will keep in airtight containers in the refrigerator for 5 days or in the freezer for 1 month.

These jam filled crunchy cookies signal the start of the holiday season.

Scottish Shortbread Triangles

Preparation Time: 15 minutes / **Chilling Time:** 30 minutes / **Baking Time:** 55 minutes

Equipment: *Two 9-inch springform pans, bottoms lined with parchment paper, a stand mixer fitted with the paddle attachment or handheld mixer.*

This is a butter rich crumbly shortbread, and the addition of brown sugar and toasted oats add a nice depth of flavor to the cookie. When baked in a springform pan, the rounds of shortbread remind me of the old-fashioned paper wrapped disks of shortbread, which you could find in the food halls of department stores. I often tie a ribbon around 3 or 4 triangles and give them away in clear bags for special treats. Note: this recipe is easily halved.

2 cups good quality
    salted butter at room
    temperature

1¾ cups packed brown sugar

1½ cups toasted large flaked
    quick oats, divided (½ cup
    of oats will be used for
    garnish)

3 cups all-purpose flour

½ cup cornstarch

¾ teaspoon salt

Evenly distribute the oats on a parchment lined baking sheet and bake for 7 minutes. When cool, whisk together 1 cup of the toasted oats, flour, cornstarch, and salt on a large piece of parchment paper.

In the bowl of the stand mixer, cream the butter, gradually adding the sugar. Beat on high speed until creamy and smooth. Reduce the speed to low and tip the dry ingredients into the butter mixture, until just combined.

Scrape the dough out onto a large piece of floured parchment paper and knead the dough a few times to make sure the flour and oats are evenly incorporated. Divide the dough in half and press half the dough evenly into each lined springform pan. Score the shortbread into 12 to 16 wedges. Prick the wedges all over with the tines of a fork. Sprinkle the rest of the toasted oats over the shortbread wedges and gently press the oats into the dough.

Refrigerate both pans of shortbread for 30 minutes, or until cold. I often place them in the freezer.

Preheat the oven to 330°F. Bake both tins on the same middle rack in the oven for approximately 55 to 60 minutes. The shortbread should be lightly browned in the center and around the edges. Let the shortbread cool for 10 minutes and while still warm in the pans, score the wedges once more. Let them cool completely before releasing the shortbread from the tins and slicing into cookies.

This shortbread keeps well in airtight containers in the cupboard or the refrigerator for up to two weeks and can be frozen for up to 3 months.

Triple Chocolate Shortbread

Preparation Time: 30 minutes / **Chilling Time:** 1 hour / **Baking Time:** 20 minutes

Equipment: *A stand mixer fitted with the paddle attachment or handheld mixer, three 12 x 18-inch parchment lined cookie sheets, 1 small to medium sized cookie cutter of your choosing (I chose a leaf).*

Delicious, elegant and a chocolate shortbread lover's dream. These cookies are distinct and look pretty in any kind of a small gift box. The combination of a good quality cocoa powder and dark chocolate intensifies the depth of chocolate without making the cookie too sweet. Finishing the cookie in milk chocolate just sends it into a chocolate world of its own. Note: this recipe is easily halved.

2 cups butter

1 cup superfine sugar

½ cup good quality unsweetened cocoa powder

3½ cups flour

4 tablespoons cornstarch

3 (100-gram) 70% chocolate bars, chopped (I used Lindt)

½ teaspoon salt

1½ cups milk chocolate Callebaut callets or Chipits or chopped chocolate for finishing.

Melt the dark chocolate in a heat proof bowl over 2 inches of simmering water in a medium saucepan. There should be no more than 2 inches of water in the saucepan. Let cool, once melted.

Whisk the flour, cornstarch, and salt together on a large piece of parchment paper. Sift in the cocoa powder and combine well. In the bowl of the stand mixer, beat the butter and sugar together until light and fluffy. With the mixer on low, stir in the cooled chocolate. Tip in the dry ingredients until just combined.

Scrape the dough out onto a floured sheet of parchment or wax paper. Knead the dough a few times to make sure you have a smooth texture. Divide the dough into 3 disks and refrigerate the dough for at least 1 hour, or longer.

Take the dough out of the refrigerator 20 minutes before you plan to roll it.

Roll the dough between 2 sheets of floured wax paper to ¼ inch thickness. Cut the dough out with a small to medium sized cookie cutter of your choosing. (I always use a leaf cutter.) Place the cookies 1-inch apart on the prepared cookie sheets.

Refrigerate the sheets of cookies once more for 1 hour before baking to ensure that they hold their shape. The cookie sheets can be stacked, one on top of another with a sheet of wax paper in between.

Preheat the oven to 325°F. Bake the cookies for 18 to 20 minutes until the cookies lose their shine. Let cool on wire racks.

FINISHING CHOCOLATE

Melt the milk chocolate in a heatproof bowl over a saucepan of simmering water. There should be no more than 2 inches of water in the saucepan. Stirring constantly, bring the chocolate to a temperature of 90°F or 32°C. The chocolate should look shiny and feel quite warm, but not hot, to the touch. Dip half of each cookie into the melted chocolate. Scrape the excess chocolate off with an offset spatula. Let the chocolate set at room temperature for approximately 2 hours, or in the refrigerator for an hour.

The cookies can be stored in airtight containers in the refrigerator for up to 2 weeks or in the freezer for up to 2 months.

Wouldn't you want to receive a box of these luscious cookies?

Shortbread Rounds with Vanilla Buttercream Icing

Preparation Time: 30 minutes/ **Chilling Time:** 1 hour/**Baking Time:** 20 minutes

Equipment: Three 12 x 18-inch baking sheets, a stand mixer fitted with a steel blade or a handheld mixer.

These shortbreads are tender and buttery and both children and adults, alike, love them. I make them for all occasions and change the icing designs, accordingly. Usually, I use a 2-inch round cookie cutter. Because I made these cookies in the summer for a children's party, I decided to make them into fish. This was achieved by placing a sour candy fish on a blue frosted background.

COOKIES

2 cups butter, room
    temperature
¾ cup fruit or superfine sugar
1 teaspoon vanilla
½ teaspoon salt
3¾ cups flour
¼ cup cornstarch

BUTTERCREAM

1 cup butter, room
    temperature
3¼ cups icing sugar
2 teaspoons vanilla extract
1 to 2 tablespoons
    whipping cream

COOKIES

Whisk together the flour, salt, and cornstarch on a large piece of parchment paper.

In the bowl of the stand mixer, cream the butter. Gradually, add the sugar until the mixture is light and fluffy. Add in the vanilla. Tip in the dry ingredients and mix together on low speed, until just combined. Do not overmix.

Scrape the dough out onto a floured piece of parchment paper. With floured hands knead the dough a few times, until smooth. Shape the dough into two disks and refrigerate for 1 hour. Remove from the refrigerator 20 minutes before you plan to roll out the dough. Between waxed paper, roll the dough to between ¼ and ⅓ inch thickness. With a floured cookie cutter, cut out shapes and place on the prepared cookie sheets 1-inch apart.

Refrigerate the cookies once more for 30 minutes to ensure they will keep their shape in the oven. You can stack the cookie sheets one on top of another with a piece of waxed paper in between.

Preheat the oven to 325°F. Bake the cookies for 20 to 25 minutes, until very lightly browned. Remove to racks and let cool completely.

BUTTERCREAM ICING

In the bowl of the stand mixer, beat the butter until creamy. Gradually add the sugar, one cup at a time. Add the vanilla and whipping cream. Beat until creamy and smooth. If you wish to color the icing, divide the icing into separate bowls and place one or two drops of organic vegetable food gel into each bowl. Spread the icing evenly over the cooled cookies or pipe the icing onto the cookies with a medium sized star tip. These cookies will keep in the refrigerator in airtight containers for 5 days or can be frozen for up to 1 month.

Have fun with these cookies. These "fish" shortbreads went to a 6-year-old's birthday party!

Persian Shortbread Cookies with Pistachios

(GLUTEN-FREE)

Preparation Time: 30 minutes / **Resting Time:** 1 hour / **Baking Time:** 15 minutes

Equipment: Two 12 x 18-inch baking sheets, lined with parchment paper, a stand mixer or handheld mixer, a small cookie cutter, traditionally in a cloverleaf shape, however, I used a small round cutter.

These Iranian cookies (Nan-e Nokhodchi) are made with toasted chickpea flour and are infused with cardamom and rose water accents. They are fragrant and crumbly in texture. Nan-e Nokhodchi are usually made to celebrate the Persian New Year and, because several households often are visited in a day, these delicate cookies are made small enough to have plenty to go around. I have added a yolk to the dough (which is not traditional) but it really helps to bring the dough together, when mixing.

1 cup plus 1 tablespoon
  butter, melted and strained
1 cup icing sugar
1 egg yolk, room temperature
2½ cups toasted
  chickpea flour
1 teaspoon cardamom
¼ teaspoon rosewater
1 teaspoon vanilla
½ teaspoon salt
½ cup very finely chopped
  toasted pistachios
  (I used a food processor)

Preheat the oven to 350°F. Spread the chickpea flour out on a parchment lined baking sheet and toast for eight minutes, stirring the flour around with a spoon at the four-minute mark. Set aside.

Melt the butter in a small saucepan on medium low heat, swirling the pan occasionally. Allow the butter to simmer until you see white solids forming on the top and bottom of the pan. You do not want the butter to brown. Remove the butter from the heat and strain it through a fine mesh sieve into the bowl of the stand mixer to remove most of the white solids. Do not worry about getting all of the white solids out.

When the butter has cooled to barely warm, add the icing sugar and beat on medium high speed until the butter and sugar form a creamy paste. Add the egg yolk, rosewater, cardamom, salt and vanilla and beat until well incorporated. Sift in the chickpea flour, one cup at a time, mixing on low after each addition. Scrape out the dough onto a chickpea floured piece of wax paper.

Using floured hands, knead and pat the dough into two disks. Cover each disk with another sheet of floured wax paper and with a rolling pin gently roll out the dough to ⅓ inch thickness. Leave the dough to rest for 1 hour at room temperature, before cutting it into shapes.

Preheat the oven to 325°F. Cut out the cookies and place the cookies one inch apart on the prepared baking sheets. Sprinkle each cookie with the finely chopped pistachios. Bake for 15 to 18 minutes, until fragrant and golden brown.

These cookies will keep in airtight containers in the refrigerator for 1 week or can be frozen for up to 2 months.

The floral scent of these cookies is very subtle but tantalizing at the same time.

Maple Leaf Cookies with Maple Syrup Glaze

Preparation Time: 15 minutes / **Chilling Time:** 2 hours / **Baking Time:** 15 to 20 minutes

Equipment: *Three 12 x 18-inch parchment lined cookie sheets, stand mixer fitted with the paddle attachment or handheld mixer, maple leaf cookie cutter.*

I always go to my local Farmers' Market in the Spring and buy a dark Grade B maple syrup to make these cookies. Without a doubt, these cookies have the deepest flavor of any maple cookies I have ever eaten and, in my most humble opinion, can compete with the maple glazed cookies they sell in Quebec City. The cookies make lovely gifts for out-of-town visitors, packaged with a small bottle of pure maple syrup.

3 cups flour

½ teaspoon baking powder

½ teaspoon salt

1 cup butter at room temperature

1 cup dark brown sugar

1 large egg plus 1 yolk at room temperature

⅔ cup maple syrup (Grade B is best if you can find it)

½ teaspoon maple extract

GLAZE

½ cup maple syrup

2 cups icing sugar

Pinch of salt

Whisk together the flour, baking powder and salt on a large sheet of parchment paper.

In the bowl of the stand mixer, cream the butter and sugar, until light. Add the whole egg and yolk and continue mixing until fluffy. With the mixer on low, gradually stream in the maple syrup and extract and beat until well incorporated. Tip in the dry ingredients until just blended. Scrape the dough out onto a floured sheet of parchment or wax paper. The dough will be quite soft. Knead the dough a few times and form the dough into two large discs. Chill the dough for 2 hours or overnight in the refrigerator. Take the dough out of the refrigerator 20 minutes before you plan to roll it out.

Roll out the dough between 2 sheets of lightly floured waxed paper to a ¼ inch thickness. Cut out the leaf shapes and place them on your prepared cookie sheets 1-inch apart. I often use one small and one medium sized leaf cutter as I think it makes for a nice presentation. Chill the cookies on the baking sheets for 30 minutes. You can stack the cookie sheets one on top of another with a piece of waxed paper in between.

Preheat the oven to 350°F. Bake the cookies for approximately 15 to 18 minutes or until golden brown. Let the cookies cool on wire racks.

GLAZE

While the cookies are cooling, make your glaze. Add 2 cups of icing sugar to ½ cup of maple syrup and stir to a smooth, creamy consistency. If the glaze is too thin, add more icing sugar, if too thick, add more maple syrup. Add a pinch of salt to taste.

Dip the top of each cookie into the glaze and let the glaze set on the cookies for 2 hours at room temperature. These cookies can be stored in airtight containers in the refrigerator for 1 week or in the freezer for 2 months.

Gingerbread Dancers with White Chocolate

Preparation Time: 15 minutes / **Chilling Time:** 2 hours / **Baking Time:** 12 minutes

Equipment: *Three 12 x 18-inch parchment lined baking sheets, stand mixer or hand-held mixer, piping bag for decoration.*

This is a must have gingerbread cookie recipe, which can be used to make cookie cut outs, gingerbread houses, or star shaped trees. The gingerbread is crisp, gingery and easy to work with when rolling into shapes. I have made gingerbread dancers and have used white chocolate, with a hint of pink food coloring, to dress up these figurines. For Christmas, I often place the gingerbread dancers on a cake or a Yule log as an added festive touch.

GINGERBREAD

1 cup butter at room
    temperature
1 cup dark brown sugar
½ cup fancy molasses
1 large egg
3½ cups flour
½ teaspoon salt
1 teaspoon baking powder
½ teaspoon baking soda
2½ teaspoons ground ginger
    (the fresher the ginger,
    the better)
1 teaspoon cinnamon
¼ teaspoon allspice

FINISHING CHOCOLATE

1½ cup of white chocolate
    Callebaut callets, Chipits
    or three 100-gram bars
    chopped good quality
    white chocolate.
Pink food coloring gel, if
    desired.

COOKIES

Whisk together the flour, salt, ginger, allspice, cinnamon, baking powder and baking soda on a large sheet of parchment paper.

In the bowl of a stand mixer, cream together the butter and the sugar until light and fluffy. Add the egg and continue to mix thoroughly. Stream in the molasses until well combined. With the mixer on low, tip in the dry ingredients. Mix until incorporated, but do not overmix. Turn the dough out onto a sheet of floured parchment or wax paper. Knead the dough a few times, then divide the dough in half and shape the dough into two round discs. Cover in plastic wrap and chill for at least 2 hours.

Take the dough out of the fridge 20 minutes before you plan to roll it. Roll the dough out between lightly floured sheets of waxed paper to a ¼ inch thickness. Flour your cutter as needed. (I place a bowl of flour beside me to dip my cutters in as I am working.) Place the cookies on the prepared baking sheets, 1½ inches apart. Chill the cookies on the sheets for 30 minutes. The baking sheets can be stacked in the refrigerator one on top of another with a sheet of wax paper in between.

Preheat the oven to 350°F. Bake the cookies for 12 to 15 minutes. Cool on wire racks.

FINISHING CHOCOLATE

Melt the chocolate in a heatproof bowl over a saucepan of simmering water. There should be no more than 2 inches of water in the saucepan. Do not allow the chocolate to get too hot as white chocolate scorches easily. When the chocolate is melted add 2 or 3 drops of food coloring to the chocolate, if using, and stir well. Pipe the chocolate onto the cooled gingerbread.

These cookies will keep in airtight containers in the refrigerator for 1 week or in the freezer for 2 months.

Peanut Butter Cream Sandwich Cookies

Preparation Time: 30 minutes / **Chilling Time:** 30 minutes / **Baking Time:** 12 to 15 minutes

Equipment: *Three 12 x 18-inch large cookie sheets, stand mixer fitted with the paddle attachment or handheld mixer, 1 medium cookie scoop.*

This is the one cookie that I simply cannot resist. I keep them in the freezer, and they are even better tasting taken straight out of the freezer than at room temperature. The secret to the filling is whipping the cream and peanut butter for a long time until it is so light that it melts in your mouth.

COOKIES

2½ cups flour

½ teaspoon salt

¾ teaspoon baking soda

1½ cups smooth conventional peanut butter (be generous)

1 cup butter

¾ cup dark brown sugar

¾ cup white sugar

1 large egg

1½ teaspoons vanilla

FOR THE FILLING

1½ cups smooth conventional peanut butter

½ cup butter

3 cups icing sugar

½ cup whipping cream

1 generous teaspoon vanilla

On a large sheet of parchment paper, whisk together the flour, salt, and baking soda.

In the bowl of the stand mixer, cream the butter, peanut butter and both sugars until light and fluffy. Add the egg and vanilla. With the mixer on low, tip in the flour until just combined. Use a medium or large sized cookie scoop to scoop the batter into balls. Place the balls of dough on the parchment lined cookie sheets, 2 inches apart. Gently press down on each cookie with the tines of a fork. Refrigerate the cookies for 30 minutes.

Preheat the oven to 360°F. Bake for 12 to 15 minutes or until golden brown. Let cool completely on wire racks.

FILLING

While the cookies are baking, prepare the filling. In the bowl of the stand mixer, cream together the butter and peanut butter until smooth. On low speed, gradually add the icing sugar. Add the vanilla to the whipping cream and slowly stream the cream into the peanut butter mixture. Increase the speed of the mixer and beat the peanut butter cream for at least 2 minutes, until it is light and velvety.

ASSEMBLY

When the cookies are cool, place 2 tablespoons of filling onto the bottom sides of half of the cookies. Top with the remaining cookies bottom side down.

Store in the refrigerator for up to 1 week or in the freezer for up to 2 months.

Squareos with Mascarpone Cream Cheese Filling

Preparation Time: 30 minutes / **Chilling Time:** 1 hour / **Baking Time:** 20 minutes

---

Equipment: *Four 12 x 18-inch parchment lined cookie sheets, stand mixer or hand-held mixer, rolling pin, square shaped 1½ inch cookie cutter, piping bag (optional).*

This cookie is like an Oreo cookie on steroids. The cookie itself consists of a melt in your mouth chocolate shortbread and the filling of mascarpone and cream cheese contrasts beautifully with the chocolate. When frozen, I eat them as if they were mini-ice cream sandwiches. They look beautiful in a chocolate box and I try to find unique boxes to fill for my friends.

COOKIES

3½ cups flour

¾ cup sifted unsweetened cocoa powder

½ teaspoon salt

2 cups butter fridge cold cut into cubes

1 cup sugar

FILLING

1 cup mascarpone cheese at room temperature

1 cup cream cheese at room temperature

½ cup sugar

1 teaspoon pure vanilla extract

Pinch of salt

COOKIES

On a large piece of parchment paper, whisk together the flour and salt and sift in the cocoa powder. In the bowl of the stand mixer, cream the butter with the sugar until the mixture is fairly smooth. Lower the speed and tip in the dry ingredients. When the flour and cocoa are fully incorporated, stop the mixer. Do not overmix. Scrape the dough out onto a large piece of floured parchment or wax paper. Knead the dough a few times before shaping into 3 round discs. Refrigerate the dough for 1 hour or longer. Take the dough out of the fridge 20 minutes before you plan to roll it.

Roll the dough out between 2 sheets of lightly floured wax paper to a thickness of ¼ inch. With a 1½ inch square cookie cutter, cut out the dough and place the cookies 1-inch apart on the cookie sheet. Continue until you have rolled out all 3 discs of dough. Chill the sheets of cookies in the fridge for 1 hour. You can stack the baking sheets one on top of another with a sheet of wax paper in between.

Preheat the oven to 325°F. Bake for 20 to 25 minutes until the cookies have lost their shine. Let cool on wire racks.

FILLING

In the bowl of a stand mixer, combine the mascarpone, cream cheese, vanilla, and sugar. Add a pinch of salt. Beat until smooth and creamy. You can also do this by hand.

ASSEMBLY

Using a piping bag or an offset spatula, place 2 teaspoons of filling on the bottom side of half the cookies. Top with the remaining cookies bottom side down.

These cookies can be refrigerated for up to 1 week and frozen for up to 2 months.

Can I say, even better than a box of chocolates?

Alfajores with Dulce de Leche

Preparation Time: 30 minutes / **Chilling Time:** 2 hours / **Baking Time:** 12 to 15 minutes

Equipment: Four 12 x 18-inch baking sheets, a stand mixer fitted with the paddle attachment or handheld mixer, a round 2-inch cookie cutter.

This cookie hails from Argentina. It typically is filled with dulce de leche and I have used a good quality store bought dulce de leche in this recipe. The shortbread cookies are very tender and what gives them their tenderness is the addition of cornstarch. I have cut down a little on the traditional amount of cornstarch as I find too much corn flour can flatten the flavor, but I have added just enough to keep the melt away texture. I have also added salted, toasted finely chopped almonds to the outside center of the cookies which serves to keep the caramel in and adds a terrific crunch factor. Note: This recipe makes a lot of cookies and can be easily halved.

COOKIES

2 cups butter, room temperature

1 cup icing sugar

2 egg yolks, room temperature

2 teaspoons pure vanilla extract

3½ cups flour, scooped and leveled

1 cup cornstarch, scooped and leveled

½ teaspoon salt

1 cup toasted almonds, finely chopped

FILLING

1 tin or jar of Dulce de Leche (you will need 1½ cups), refrigerated

COOKIES

On a large sheet of parchment paper, whisk together the flour, cornstarch, and salt.

In the bowl of the stand mixer, cream together the butter and icing sugar until light and fluffy. Add the egg yolks, one at a time, beating after each addition. Tip the dry ingredients into the butter mixture and mix on low speed until just incorporated. The dough will be quite soft and sticky. Scrape the dough out onto a floured sheet of parchment or wax paper and divide the dough equally into two disks. Refrigerate the disks for 2 hours. Take the dough out of the refrigerator 20 minutes before you plan to roll it. Roll the dough between two sheets of lightly floured waxed paper to ¼ inch thickness.

Using a 2-inch cookie cutter, cut out rounds and place the cookies on the prepared sheets two inches apart. Chill the sheets of cookies for

30 minutes. Stack the cookie sheets one on top of another with a piece of waxed paper in between the sheets.

Preheat the oven to 350°F. Bake the cookies for 12 to 15 minutes. Do not let them color, they should be fully baked, but not golden brown. Allow them to cool before filling.

FILLING

Briefly whisk the dulce de leche in the bowl of the stand mixer or by hand, in order to make it easier to spread, prior to using.

TOASTED ALMONDS

Place the almonds on a parchment lined baking sheet and toss with ¼ teaspoon salt. Toast in a 350°F oven for 6 to 7 minutes or until golden brown. Finely chop the almonds by hand or give them a whiz in a food processor. Place in a bowl and set aside.

ASSEMBLY

Place 2 teaspoons of cold dulce de leche on the bottom side of half of the cookies and top with the remaining cookies, bottom side down. Roll the outside middle of each cookie in the chopped almonds. Place in the freezer or refrigerator to set for 30 minutes. These cookies can be stored in airtight containers in the refrigerator for 5 days or can be frozen for up to 2 months.

Alfajores with Dulce de Leche

Vanilla Bean Shorties with Raspberry Buttercream

Preparation Time: 30 minutes / **Chilling Time:** 1 hour / **Baking Time:** 20 minutes

---

Equipment: *Three to four 12 x 18-inch parchment lined baking sheets, stand mixer or hand mixer, daisy cookie cutter or cookie cutter of your choice, rolling pin, piping bag (optional).*

These sandwich cookies are a staple for bringing to afternoon teas—they just look so pretty on a serving plate! The buttery crumb of the shortbread goes wonderfully with the raspberry filling, which is made with a fresh raspberry puree. The cookies also are delicious served as single biscuits with a pot of jam and a cup of tea.

COOKIES
- 2 cups butter
- 1 cup superfine sugar
- 3¾ cups flour
- ¼ cup cornstarch
- ½ teaspoon salt
- Scraped seeds from
  - 1 vanilla bean pod *or*
  - 1 heaping teaspoon of vanilla bean paste

RASPBERRY PUREE
(for Filling)
- ½ cup good quality seedless raspberry jam
- 1½ cups fresh raspberries
- ½ cup sugar
- 1 teaspoon lemon juice
- 1 tablespoon Chambord Raspberry liqueur (optional)

BUTTERCREAM
(for Filling)
- 1¼ cups butter
- 4 cups icing sugar
- 1 teaspoon vanilla
- 2 tablespoons whipping cream
- ½ cup raspberry puree

COOKIES

On a large sheet of parchment paper, whisk together the flour, cornstarch, and salt.

In the bowl of the stand mixer, cream together the butter and sugar until light and fluffy. Add the scraped seeds from the vanilla bean or the vanilla bean paste.

With the mixer on low, tip in the dry ingredients and mix until just incorporated. Scrape the dough out onto a floured sheet of parchment or wax paper and knead a few times. Form the dough into 3 round disks. Refrigerate the disks for at least 1 hour or longer. Bring the disks out of the refrigerator 20 minutes before you plan to roll the dough. Roll out the disks of dough between floured sheets of waxed paper to ¼ inch thickness.

Using a floured 1½ inch daisy or round cutter, cut out the shapes and place on the prepared cookie sheets, 1-inch apart. Chill the sheets of cookies for 30 minutes. You can stack the cookie sheets one on top of another with a piece of wax paper in between.

Preheat the oven to 325°F. Bake the cookies for 20 to 25 minutes or until just light golden in color. Cool on racks.

RASPBERRY PUREE

This can be prepared up to three days ahead of time. In a small saucepan, heat the raspberry jam. Add the fresh raspberries, lemon juice, sugar, and the Chambord liqueur, if using. Bring the jam to a low boil for 5 minutes, stirring occasionally to break up the fresh raspberries. Strain the puree into a heat proof bowl and return the puree to the saucepan. Bring to a boil once more and allow the jam to boil for 5 minutes, until slightly reduced and thickened. Remove from the heat. Tip into a container and place in the refrigerator or freezer to cool.

BUTTERCREAM

Cream the butter and icing sugar together in the bowl of the stand mixer until well incorporated. Add in the vanilla. Begin to stream in the raspberry puree. You can start with ½ cup and if you want more of a raspberry flavor, add another ¼ cup. Beat the icing on medium speed until the jam is fully incorporated. With the mixer on low, add the cream and beat again on medium speed until you have a smooth, velvety consistency. Add a pinch of salt to taste.

ASSEMBLY

With an offset spatula or piping bag, place 2 teaspoons of the buttercream on the bottom side of half the cookies. Top with the remaining cookies, bottom side down. These cookies will keep in airtight containers in the refrigerator for 1 week or in the freezer for 2 months.

Chocolate Crinkle Cookies
with Caramel Cream

Preparation Time: 30 minutes / **Chilling Time:** 2 hours / **Baking Time:** 15 minutes

Equipment: *A stand mixer fitted with a paddle attachment, three 12 x 18-inch baking sheets lined with parchment paper, a piping bag for filling the cookies (optional).*

The chocolate crunch in this cookie contrasts beautifully with a lighter textured caramel cream filling. The caramel is made by heating a sugar syrup to a rich amber stage and then adding whipping cream and butter. When cooled it is whipped up into a caramel cream. Did I say "lighter" filling, well I meant lighter as in airy, not lighter as in calories. When I bring these cookies to work, they disappear within five minutes.

COOKIES

2¼ cups flour

¾ cup unsweetened cocoa powder

2 teaspoons baking soda

½ teaspoon salt

1 cup butter at room temperature

1 cup brown sugar

½ cup white sugar

2 large eggs, room temperature

1 teaspoon vanilla

1 cup icing sugar (for the balls of cookie
   dough to be rolled in)

CARAMEL CREAM

2 cups sugar

¼ cup water

2 teaspoons corn syrup

1 cup warmed whipping cream

½ cup butter cut into cubes

½ teaspoon salt

COOKIES

On a large piece of parchment paper, whisk together the flour, baking soda and salt. Sift the cocoa into the flour mixture and combine well. In the bowl of a stand mixer, cream together the butter and both sugars, until light. Add the eggs one at a time and beat until the mixture is fluffy. Add the vanilla. On low speed, tip in the dry ingredients and mix until just combined. Scrape the dough out into a large mixing bowl and refrigerate the dough in the mixing bowl for 2 hours.

Bring the bowl out of the refrigerator 20 minutes before scooping the cookies.

Recipe continues on the next page

Preheat the oven to 350°F. With a medium or large sized cookie scoop, scoop the dough into balls. Place the icing sugar into a bowl. Roll each ball in the icing sugar until very well coated. Place on the prepared cookie sheets 2 inches apart. Bake for 15 to 20 minutes.

CARAMEL CREAM

Place the sugar in a medium sized saucepan. Pour the water over the sugar and swirl the pan gently to evenly distribute the water. Add the corn syrup to the sugar mixture.

Heat the sugar on medium high heat until the sugar has completely dissolved. Bring the syrup to a boil and allow to boil, stirring only occasionally, for approximately 6 to 7 minutes. When the syrup reaches a deep amber color, take it off the heat.

Warm the whipping cream in the microwave for 30 seconds and add it to the caramel syrup, stirring until the syrup becomes smooth. It will boil up so be careful.

Take the caramel off the heat once more and stir in the butter. Allow the caramel to cool in the refrigerator, uncovered. The caramel will thicken as it cools. When cold, place the caramel in the bowl of a stand mixer and beat on medium high speed until thick and velvety.

ASSEMBLY

Place one tablespoon of caramel cream on half the cookies, bottom side up. Sandwich with the remaining cookies, bottom side down. These cookies will keep in airtight containers in the refrigerator for 1 week or in the freezer for 2 months.

Hazelnut Linzer Cookies
with Raspberry Jam

Preparation Time: 30 minutes / **Chilling Time:** 2 hours / **Baking Time:** 20 to 25 minutes

Equipment: *Three 12 x 18-inch parchment lined cookie sheets, a stand mixer or handheld mixer, a round cookie cutter, a much smaller round cookie cutter for the holes, a rolling pin.*

I love Linzer cookies and find their nutty flavor, combined with the traditional filling of raspberry jam, irresistible. I cannot pass by a bakery featuring Linzer cookies behind a glass counter, without stopping in and buying one. There is something so compelling and satisfying about this confection. This recipe features hazelnut, rather than almond in the cookie wafers, but the cookie is delicious with either. With a small cookie cutter, I have cut out a hole in the center of half the cookies to reveal the gorgeous red raspberry jam.

COOKIES

1½ cups hazelnut flour or finely chopped hazelnuts (lightly toasted in a 350°F oven for 7 minutes)

2 cups flour

1 teaspoon cinnamon

½ teaspoon baking powder

2 teaspoons grated lemon rind

½ teaspoon salt

1¼ cups butter, room temperature

¾ cup white sugar

1 egg plus 1 yolk, room temperature

1 teaspoon vanilla

2 tablespoon of icing sugar for dusting

FILLING

1 cup seedless raspberry jam plus 1 teaspoon of lemon juice and 1 tablespoon of Chambord liqueur (optional)

COOKIES

Whisk together the two flours, cinnamon, baking powder and salt on a large sheet of parchment paper. In the bowl of a stand mixer cream the butter and sugar until light and fluffy. Add the egg and the yolk and beat on medium speed until the mixture is smooth. Add the lemon zest. With the mixer on low, tip in the dry ingredients until the flour is just combined. Scrape out the dough onto a piece of floured parchment or wax paper. Knead the dough a few times and then form the dough into 2 round discs. The dough will be quite sticky for a cookie dough.

Wrap the disks in plastic wrap and refrigerate for at least 2 hours. Take the disks of dough out of the fridge 20 minutes before you plan to roll the dough.

Roll the dough between floured sheets of wax paper to ¼ inch thickness. With a 2-inch round plain or fluted cookie cutter, cut out the cookies. Using a small round cookie cutter, cut the centers out of half of the cookies. Place the tops of the cookies on the same baking sheet as they will take slightly less time to bake. Refrigerate the sheets of cookies for 30 minutes. The sheets can be stacked in the refrigerator one on top of another with a sheet of waxed paper in between.

Preheat the oven to 350°F. Bake the bottom cookies for 20 to 25 minutes or until the cookies are nicely browned and fragrant. The tops of the cookies will take about 5 to 7 minutes less time to bake. Let cool on wire racks.

FILLING

Microwave the jam for 30 seconds to loosen it up, then give it a good stir with the lemon juice and liqueur, if using. Let the jam cool to a spreadable consistency.

ASSEMBLY

Spread 1 heaping teaspoon of jam on each cookie bottom and top with the cutout center cookies. Place the sandwich cookies on a baking sheet and place the sheet in the freezer for ½ hour in order for the jam to set. Remove the cookies and dust with icing sugar. These cookies will keep in airtight containers in the refrigerator for 1 week or in the freezer for 2 months.

Chocolate Dipped Palmiers or Elephant Ears

Preparation Time: 25 minutes / **Chilling Time:** 30 minutes / **Baking Time:** 12 to 15 minutes

Equipment: *Two 12 x 18-inch parchment lined baking sheets, 2 offset spatulas, large cutting board.*

These cookies remind me of Paris, where they are featured in all the bakeries. The name "Palmier" comes from its shape which means palm leaf in French, but in North America they often are referred to as "Elephant Ears." This recipe makes small palmiers, which I find nicer to present as gifts. I use store bought butter puff pastry to make these cookies, which makes the process of making and shaping the palmiers much more baker friendly. I dip one side of the palmier in dark chocolate. I got this idea when I had the occasion to eat in a very fancy restaurant, where they dipped their palmiers in chocolate and then served them with blackcurrant ice cream for dessert. Unfortunately, I could not find blackcurrant ice cream when I made these cookies, however, they were terrific on their own.

2 cups white sugar

2 heaping tablespoons of cinnamon

½ teaspoon salt

1 package or 2 sheets store bought butter puff pastry, thawed according to package instructions, but must be cold when used.

1½ cups chopped dark chocolate, or Callebaut callets, for dipping

Whisk together the sugar, cinnamon and salt in a medium size bowl. Spread ½ cup of the sugar mixture evenly over a large cutting board. Place the first sheet of puff pastry onto the sugared board and roll it out to a 12- to 13-inch square. Make sure the pastry is being evenly pressed into the sugar. Generously sprinkle the top of the puff pastry with another ½ cup of the sugar mixture.

To make the elephant ear shape, fold the 2 sides of the square (the sides to the left and right of you as you are facing the pastry) into the middle of the square. Now there is a seam where the 2 sides of the pastry meet in the center. Next, fold each side once more into the center of the square.

Press down lightly on the folds. This will help the elephant ears keep their shape while baking. Now fold one half of the pastry over the other half as though closing a book and lightly press the 2 halves of pastry together. You should have 8 layers of puff pastry in a log shape with one outside opening seam.

With a very sharp knife, with the seam of the log facing away from you, slice the log into ⅓ inch slices and place the palmiers on the prepared cookie sheets 1½ inches apart. Place the sheet of cookies in the refrigerator or freezer to chill for 30 minutes and begin to prepare the next sheet of puff pastry.

Continue with the next sheet of puff pastry as you did for the first, following the same directions as above to make the elephant ear shape. Slice the log into cookies and place the second batch of palmiers on a prepared baking sheet and refrigerate for 30 minutes.

Preheat the oven to 425°F. Take the first sheet of palmiers out of the refrigerator and bake in the middle of the oven for approximately 6 minutes. As they caramelize, the cookies may need to be tidied up to maintain their shape. Simply take the palmiers out of the oven, and close the tips, using an offset spatula or tongs. Note: You also can insert a toothpick into each cookie just above the base of the cookie to keep the folds together, while baking. After tidying, flip the cookies over for even caramelization and bake for another 6 to 8 minutes. The palmiers should be golden brown in color. Remove from the oven and let cool completely. Start with the next batch.

FINISHING CHOCOLATE

Place the chocolate in a heat proof bowl above a saucepan of simmering water. There should be no more than 2 inches of water in the saucepan. Stir the chocolate until melted. The chocolate should feel warm to the touch and reach a temperature of 90°F or 32°C. Dip half of each cookie into the chocolate and allow the chocolate to set at room temperature for two hours or in the refrigerator for 1 hour. These cookies can be refrigerated for 2 weeks or can be frozen for up to 2 months.

These cookies make an elegant dessert served with a tangy fruit ice cream or sorbet.

Lemon Explosion Cookies

Preparation Time: 20 minutes / **Chilling Time:** 2 hours / **Baking Time:** 20 minutes

Equipment: *Food processor fitted with a steel blade, three 12 x 18-inch baking sheets lined with parchment paper.*

This cookie is a lemon lover's dream. It has an abundance of lemon flavor from both the lemon zested sugar and the freshly squeezed lemon juice in the dough. But what really tops the citrus scale is the tangy lemon glaze.

COOKIES

1½ cups white sugar

3 tablespoons finely grated lemon zest

3½ cups flour

½ teaspoon salt

½ teaspoon baking powder

1½ cups cold butter, cubed

4 tablespoons lemon juice

1 teaspoon vanilla extract

2 large egg yolks

GLAZE

2 tablespoons cream cheese, room temperature

⅓ cup lemon juice

3 cups icing sugar

Pinch of salt

COOKIES

On a large piece of parchment paper, whisk together the flour, salt, and baking powder.

In the bowl of the food processor, pulse the lemon zest and the sugar until the sugar is damp and fragrant. Tip in the flour, salt and baking powder and pulse, intermittently, for about 2 seconds each time, to combine the flour.

Scatter the cold cubed butter over the flour and sugar mixture and pulse until just combined. In a separate small bowl, whisk together the egg yolks, lemon juice and vanilla. With the food processor running, stream this mixture into the flour mixture. Pulse just until the dough comes together.

Scrape the dough out onto a floured piece of parchment paper. Knead the dough a few times to bring it together into a smooth round disk. Divide the dough into two and make two logs, approximately 10 inches long. Wrap the logs in plastic wrap and refrigerate for at least 2 hours or overnight.

Preheat the oven to 360°F. Slice the logs into ¼ to ⅓ inch slices. Place on the prepared cookie sheets 1½ inches apart. Bake for approximately 20 minutes until golden in color. Cool completely on wire racks.

GLAZE

In a medium size bowl, whisk together the softened cream cheese, lemon juice, icing sugar and a pinch of salt.

ASSEMBLY

Spoon the glaze on the top of each cookie and let the glaze set at room temperature for 1 hour or in the refrigerator for 30 minutes.

These cookies will keep in airtight containers in the refrigerator for 5 days or in the freezer for 2 months.

Jam Jar Cookies

Preparation Time: 20 minutes / **Chilling Time:** 1 hour / **Baking Time:** 20 minutes

Equipment: *A stand mixer fitted with the paddle attachment, or handheld mixer, two 12 x 18-inch baking sheets lined with parchment paper.*

Basically, this recipe involves spooning your choice of jam into a groove (made by a wooden spoon handle) on the top of a log of shortbread. The log is then cut into cookies. This is Carlin's, my middle daughter, favorite cookie. It is not the most beautiful cookie, having a somewhat rustic look with the jam spilling over onto the shortbread, however, the buttery taste of the shortbread mixed with a lovely tasting jam more than compensates for a less than elegant presentation. This recipe makes four 8-inch logs.

1 cup butter at room
  temperature

½ cup white sugar

1 teaspoon vanilla extract

2 cups flour

¼ teaspoon salt

½ cup seedless raspberry
  jam or jam of your choice,
  warmed in the microwave
  to loosen and mixed with
  1 teaspoon of lemon juice

In the bowl of the stand mixer fitted with the paddle attachment, cream together the butter and sugar until very light and fluffy. Add the vanilla and salt. With the mixer on very low speed, tip in the flour, 1 cup at a time, until all the flour is incorporated. Do not overmix.

Scrape out the dough onto a large piece of floured parchment or wax paper and knead a few times. Divide the dough evenly into four pieces. Shape each piece into an 8-inch log, approximately 2 inches wide. Press a wooden spoon handle lengthwise down the center of each log to make a shallow long groove. Fill the groove with jam. I tend to make a somewhat deeper and wider groove than the actual shape of the wooden spoon handle by moving the handle in a circular motion to hollow out the shortbread even more. I just can't get enough of a good quality fruit jam! However, you have to be careful not to get too close to the bottom of the log or the finished bars will break apart. Place 2 logs on each prepared cookie sheet. Refrigerate for one hour.

Preheat the oven to 335°F. Bake the logs for 25 minutes. The shortbread will be golden brown, and the jam will be bubbly. If you would like to add more jam to the groove, halfway through baking, simply remove the logs from the oven, add the jam and replace. I routinely do this with these cookies. While still warm, slice the logs into ⅓ to ½ inch thick bars.

These bars will keep in airtight containers in the refrigerator for 1 week or in the freezer for up to 2 months.

Butterscotch Crunch Cookies

Preparation Time: 20 minutes / **Chilling Time:** 2 hours / **Baking Time:** 15 minutes

Equipment: *Two 12 x 18-inch cookie sheets, lined with parchment paper, a stand mixer fitted with the paddle attachment or handheld mixer.*

This is a fairly simple slice and bake recipe, but timeless in its popularity. The addition of brown sugar and toffee creates the distinctive butterscotch flavor. These cookies are perfect to bring to school events or fundraisers as the recipe is easily tripled, they can be easily packaged and have a long shelf life.

1 cup butter

1 cup brown sugar

1 egg yolk

1 teaspoon pure vanilla extract

2½ cups flour

¼ teaspoon salt

¼ teaspoon baking powder

¾ cup Skor toffee bits

3 tablespoons turbinado sugar (I use Plantation raw sugar)

Lightly flour the toffee bits and place them in the freezer until ready to use.

On a large piece of parchment paper, whisk together the flour, salt, and baking powder.

In the bowl of the stand mixer, cream together the butter and sugar. Add the egg yolk and vanilla and continue beating until the mixture is light and fluffy. Tip in the dry ingredients and mix until just incorporated. Add in the toffee bits.

Scrape the dough out onto a floured piece of parchment paper. Knead the dough a few times and then divide it into two equal parts. Make each part into a rectangular log approximately 8 x 2 inches. I use a bench scraper to help square off the sides of the dough. Wrap the logs in plastic wrap and refrigerate for 2 hours or longer.

Preheat the oven to 350°F. Cut the logs into ⅓ inch slices and bake for 15 to 18 minutes or until golden brown. These cookies will keep in airtight containers in the refrigerator for 2 weeks or in the freezer for up to 2 months.

Chocolate Orange Butter Cookies

Preparation Time: 20 minutes / **Chilling Time:** 2 hours / **Baking Time:** 20 minutes

Equipment: *A stand mixer fitted with the paddle attachment or handheld mixer, three 12 x 18-inch cookie sheets, lined with parchment paper.*

This cookie is eye catching and incorporates two well-loved traditional flavors, chocolate and orange. The addition of brown sugar lends a caramel dimension to the cookie, which again blends well with the orange notes. Note: This recipe can easily be halved but really do you want to as you can make lots of friends with these.

2 cups salted butter

1½ cups brown sugar

2 tablespoons finely grated orange zest

2 teaspoons of vanilla extract

1 egg plus 1 yolk at room temperature

4 cups flour

½ teaspoon salt

2 cups dark 54% Callebaut callets or Chipits or four 100-gram bars of good quality dark Chocolate, chopped

Whisk together the flour and salt on a large sheet of parchment paper.

Place the brown sugar in a small bowl and add the zest, stirring until the zest is mixed well into the sugar. Cream the butter and zested sugar in the bowl of the stand mixer. With the mixer on low, add the egg and then the yolk, beating well after each addition. Add the vanilla. Stop the mixer and tip in the dry ingredients. Mix until just incorporated. Scrape the dough out onto a large piece of floured parchment.

Knead the dough a few times and bring the dough together into a smooth round ball. Shape the dough into three 12-inch round logs. Wrap in plastic wrap and refrigerate for at least 2 hours or overnight.

Preheat the oven to 325°F. Slice the logs into ¼ to ⅓ inch thick rounds. Place 1-inch apart on the baking sheets. Bake for 20 to 25 minutes or until firm and very lightly browned. Let cool on racks.

FINISHING CHOCOLATE

Place the chocolate in a heatproof bowl over a saucepan of simmering water. The water in the saucepan should not exceed a depth of 2 inches. Melt the chocolate over medium low heat, stirring all the while. When the chocolate reaches a temperature of about 32°C or 90°F, remove from the heat. It should feel warm to the touch and be thick and glossy looking. Dip half of each cooled cookie into the melted chocolate. Sprinkle with sea salt and orange zest. These cookies can be kept in airtight containers in the refrigerator for 2 weeks or in the freezer for 2 months.

Bring these to work and you will never lose your day job.

Shortbread Clouds

Preparation Time: 15 minutes / **Chilling Time:** 30 minutes / **Baking Time:** 20 minutes

Equipment: *Three 12 x 18-inch parchment lined baking sheets, stand mixer fitted with the paddle attachment or handheld mixer, one small cookie scoop.*

This recipe is unique in that it is unusual to find a traditional tasting shortbread in a drop cookie form. Most shortbread is either rolled and then cut into cookies or shaped into rectangles or rounds. The cookie has a buttery, slightly sandy texture, and the addition of Callebaut milk chocolate callets (you can substitute Chipits) provides a deliciously smooth contrast to this texture. I use a small scoop to portion out the balls of dough and the smaller size just adds to the tenderness of the cookie. The cookies are finished with roughly chopped pieces of dark chocolate. I used a 70% Lindt chocolate bar.

2 cups salted butter at room temperature

1 cup superfine, fruit or castor sugar (grind regular sugar in a food processor, if you do not have superfine sugar)

3¼ cups flour

½ cup rice flour

½ teaspoon salt

2 cups Callebaut milk chocolate callets (you can substitute Chipits)

1 dark 70% good quality chocolate bar roughly chopped into ¼ inch pieces for decorating the top of the cookies

Whisk both flours and salt together on a large piece of parchment paper.

In the bowl of the stand mixer, cream the butter and sugar together until light and fluffy.

With the mixer on low, tip the flour into the butter mixture. Mix until just combined then add the chocolate callets or Chipits.

With a small size cookie scoop, scoop balls of dough onto the baking sheets, one inch apart. Decorate the top of each cookie with a piece of chopped chocolate. I like cutting the pieces in rough triangular shapes about ¼ inch in size. Chill the sheets of cookies in the refrigerator for 30 minutes to prevent spreading in the oven.

Preheat the oven to 325°F. Bake the cookies for 20 to 25 minutes or until pale golden brown around the edges. Remove the cookies to wire racks for cooling. When cool, you can sprinkle the cookies with icing sugar or leave plain.

These cookies will keep for up to 2 weeks in the refrigerator, and up to 3 months in the freezer. This makes them a great bake ahead occasion cookie or gift.

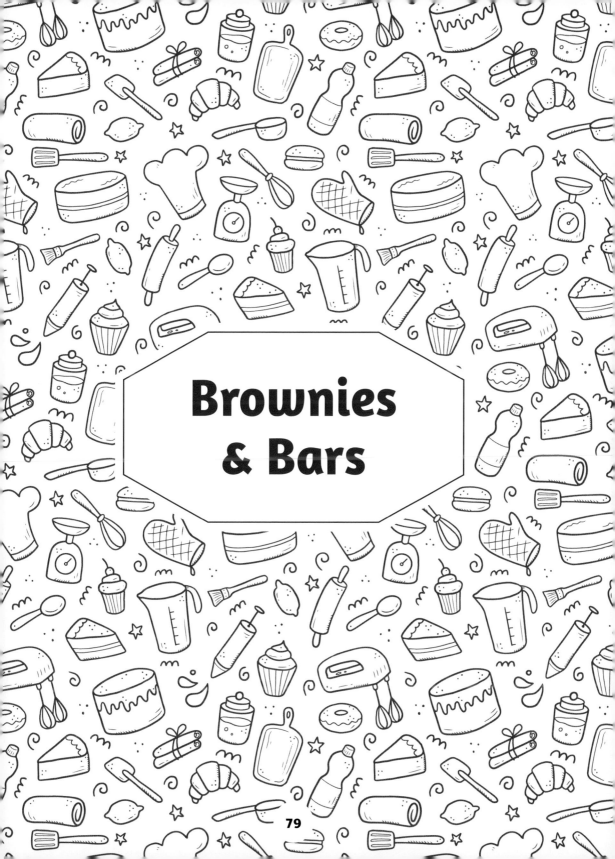

Brownies
& Bars

Halva Brownies with Tahini Chocolate Drizzle

Preparation Time: 30 minutes / **Baking Time:** 23 to 25 minutes

Equipment: *Stand mixer fitted with the whisk attachment or handheld mixer, one 9-inch square pan, lined with parchment paper.*

I first tasted halva when I was 9 years old. At first bite, I fell in love with the sweet but savory taste and layered texture of this confection. To me, it was the most exotic candy that I had ever tasted. Halva consists of a mixture of tahini (sesame seed paste) and honey or tahini and a sugar syrup. You can buy ready-made halva at boutique grocery stores. If you cannot get halva and/or do not like the taste, feel free to skip it altogether in this recipe. The brownies still will have an exceptional flavor. The tahini chocolate drizzle is easy to make and simply complements the rest of the ingredients.

THE BROWNIES

1¼ cups butter melted

2 cups good quality 60 to 70% dark chopped chocolate (you will need four 100-gram bars)

4 large eggs at room temperature

1½ cups white sugar

1 generous teaspoon vanilla

1 cup flour

⅓ cup unsweetened cocoa powder

½ teaspoon salt

1 cup broken up pieces of halva (broken into ⅓ inch pieces)

TAHINI CHOCOLATE DRIZZLE

4 tablespoons butter

4 tablespoons tahini (found in bulk and Health food stores)

4 tablespoons corn syrup

1½ cup dark 54% Callebaut chocolate callets or Chipits or chopped chocolate (you will need three 100-gram bars)

2 tablespoons hot water

Preheat the oven to 375°F. Melt the butter and chocolate together in a saucepan over low heat. Once melted, remove from the heat, and set aside, stirring occasionally until you have a thick shiny sauce. In the bowl of the stand mixer, whisk the eggs and sugar together until thick and pale in color. Add the vanilla, then the cooled chocolate mixture and mix on low speed until blended.

On a large piece of parchment paper, whisk together the flour and salt. Sift in the cocoa powder and combine. Tip the dry ingredients into the bowl of the stand mixer and mix until just incorporated. Remove the bowl from its stand and gently fold the pieces of halva into the batter. Scrape the batter into the prepared pan.

Bake for 25 minutes until the middle has a slight wobble but the brownies are set along the edges. Remove from the oven and place the pan on a wire cake rack to cool.

TAHINI CHOCOLATE DRIZZLE

Combine all the ingredients in a small heavy bottom saucepan. Whisk the ingredients over a medium low heat until you have a smooth shiny sauce. Drizzle over the cooled brownies.

These brownies will keep in airtight containers in the refrigerator for 5 days or in the freezer for 1 month.

Cheesecake Brownies

Preparation Time: 20 minutes / **Baking Time:** 30 minutes

Equipment: *A stand mixer fitted with a paddle attachment or handheld mixer, one 9-inch square baking pan, buttered and lined with parchment paper, a food processor fitted with a steel blade.*

Delightfully sweet and tangy at the same time, these brownies satisfy so many different taste buds. The cream cheese contrasts beautifully with the chocolate base giving the brownie heavenly vanilla notes and a lush texture. The brownies transport well and are perfect for school bake sales and fundraisers.

Often the first to go at fundraisers and bake sales.

BROWNIE LAYER

½ cup plus 2 tablespoons of butter, melted

¾ cup white sugar

1½ cups chopped good quality dark 70% chocolate (about three 100-gram bars)

2 tablespoons cocoa powder, unsweetened

4 large eggs at room temperature

¾ cup flour, spooned and leveled

1 teaspoon vanilla extract

½ teaspoon salt

CHEESECAKE LAYER

1 block of cream cheese (250 grams) at room temperature

2 tablespoons sour cream

1 large egg plus 1 yolk at room temperature

⅓ cup white sugar

Pinch of salt

A generous teaspoon of vanilla extract

BROWNIE LAYER

Melt the butter in a medium saucepan and add the chopped chocolate, stirring until melted and smooth.

Remove from the heat and whisk in the sugar. Break the eggs up in a bowl and whisk in a third of the eggs at a time into the chocolate mixture. Add the vanilla extract and salt. Sift in the cocoa powder and add the flour, blending until incorporated.

Reserve half a cup of the brownie batter to make a swirl pattern on top of the cheesecake layer. Pour the rest of the brownie batter into the bottom of the prepared pan and refrigerate while you make the cheesecake layer.

CHEESECAKE LAYER

Preheat the oven to 350°F. In the bowl of the food processor, pulse the cream cheese, gradually adding the sugar until incorporated. Add the egg and the yolk one at a time, pulsing after each addition. Add the vanilla extract, a pinch of salt and the sour cream and pulse until smooth. Pour the cheesecake layer evenly over the brownie mixture, using an offset spatula to spread to the corners.

SWIRL TOPPING

Mix the reserved chocolate batter with 1 tablespoon of hot water. Evenly dollop the chocolate batter over the cheesecake layer. With a knife, or the blade of an offset spatula, swirl through the dollops to create a pretty pattern.

These brownies will keep in airtight containers in the refrigerator for 4 days or in the freezer for 1 month.

Espresso Brown Butter Blondies

Preparation Time: 20 minutes / **Baking Time:** 25 minutes

Equipment: *Stand mixer fitted with the paddle attachment, or handheld mixer, a 13 x 9-inch cake pan, lined with parchment paper and buttered.*

It is hard to compete with a rich chocolate brownie, but this blondie recipe definitely is a contender. With white chocolate, Skor bar pieces, toasted walnuts and a hint of espresso, these bars can hold their own at any dessert table. The butter in these brownies is browned, which deepens the caramel notes.

1 cup butter melted and browned.

1 cup dark brown sugar

½ cup white sugar

1 tablespoon instant espresso powder

2 teaspoons vanilla extract

2 eggs plus 1 yolk at room temperature

2¼ cups flour

½ teaspoon salt

¾ teaspoon baking powder

1½ cups white chocolate Callebaut callets or Chipits

1 cup toasted walnuts, chopped

1 cup chopped Skor bars, approximately four 40-gram bars

Toast the walnuts on a lined baking sheet at 350°F for 8 minutes and give them a rough chop. Chop up the Skor bars into ¼ inch pieces, very lightly flour and place in the freezer.

In a small saucepan, melt the butter and continue cooking on medium heat until the butter begins to turn brown and smells fragrant. Continue cooking just until the butter is a uniformly brown color. Remove from the heat and allow to cool. You can place the butter in the refrigerator or freezer until ready to use.

On a large sheet of parchment paper, whisk together the flour, salt, baking powder and espresso powder. In the bowl of the stand mixer, cream together the cooled melted butter and the sugar until light and fluffy. There will be brown sediments at the bottom of the butter which is just fine to add to the bowl. Add the eggs, yolk and vanilla and beat until the mixture is smooth. Tip in the dry ingredients and mix until just blended. With the mixer on low, add the white chocolate callets or Chipits, the walnuts and Skor bar pieces.

Preheat the oven to 350°F. Scrape the batter into the prepared pan and bake for approximately 25 minutes or until browned and a toothpick inserted in the center comes out moist but clean. Allow it to cool completely before cutting into bars. These brownies can be kept in airtight containers in the refrigerator for 5 days or in the freezer for 1 month.

Armagnac Date Squares

Preparation Time: 20 minutes / **Baking Time:** 50 minutes

Equipment: *One 9-inch square pan lined with buttered parchment paper. If you would like a thinner date square, you can use a slightly larger baking pan. Just make sure it is buttered and lined well.*

These date squares are not cloyingly sweet. I have added 4 tablespoons of cognac (you can use brandy) to the simmering dates which tends to cut the sweetness. The dates are cooked in orange juice to not only enhance their flavor, but also to smooth out their texture. I was never a lover of date squares until I found a way to ramp up the flavor and work with their natural sugar content. If making for children, the alcohol can be omitted, and equal amounts of orange juice substituted. As a bonus, these bars can be considered good for you with the whole grain oats in the crisp topping, the antioxidants in the dates and the Vitamin C in the orange juice. (You can tell yourself anything.)

FILLING

4 cups Medjool Dates or 2 pounds (I buy them at Costco)

1½ cups orange juice

2 teaspoons of finely grated orange zest

2 tablespoons of lemon juice

4 tablespoons of Armagnac or brandy of your choice (optional)

1 tablespoon of dark brown sugar

1 teaspoon of vanilla

½ teaspoon of baking soda

Pinch of salt

CRISP

2 cups large flaked quick oats

1 cup flour

1 cup brown sugar

1 cup butter at room temperature

½ teaspoon cinnamon

½ teaspoon salt

¼ teaspoon baking powder

PRE-PREP
Preheat oven to 350°F.

DATE FILLING

Remove the pits and any remaining stems from the dates. Give the dates a rough chop. Place in a large saucepan and cover with the orange juice. Add the cognac or brandy, if using, the lemon juice, orange juice, zest, and brown sugar. Simmer the dates on medium high heat, stirring all the while, for approximately 7 to 10 minutes or until the dates have fallen apart and absorbed most of the liquid. Add the baking soda and stir for one more minute. The mixture should be smooth and have absorbed all the liquid. Take the dates off the heat and let cool.

CRUMBLE

In a large mixing bowl, combine the oats, flour, salt, cinnamon, and baking powder. Mix in the brown sugar, making sure there are no lumps. Cut the softened butter into cubes and begin to incorporate the butter into the flour mixture, stirring with a large spoon. This job sometimes is made easier by going right into the bowl with floured hands. When the mixture still is crumbly and the butter is evenly dispersed, spread half the crumble on the bottom of the prepared pan. Press it evenly and firmly into the sides and corners of the pan with the bottom of a glass or your hands. Spread the date filling over the crumble base. Top the date filling with the rest of the crumble and press down lightly. Bake for 50 to 55 minutes until the crisp is golden brown.

Let cool on a wire rack, then refrigerate for at least 4 hours, or overnight, before cutting into squares.

The squares will keep in airtight containers in the refrigerator for 5 days or in the freezer for 1 month.

Billionaire Bars

Preparation Time: 30 minutes / **Baking Time:** 25 minutes / **Chilling Time:** 30 minutes

Equipment: *One 9-inch square baking pan, greased and lined with parchment paper, a stand mixer fitted with the paddle attachment or handheld mixer. Please note: You also can use a 9x 13-inch pan, however the squares or chocolate bars will be thinner. Digital read thermometer recommended.*

Have you ever met anyone that did not like a shortbread caramel bar topped with chocolate? I have made these bars many, many times and they seem to be a universal favorite. You can simply top the pan of bars with chocolate and cut them into squares, or you can make the bars into mini chocolate bars and individually dip each piece into a saucepan of chocolate. It is best to have an elongated, two-pronged fork when you are doing this.

SHORTBREAD CRUST

1 cup butter

½ cup icing sugar

2 cups flour

1 teaspoon vanilla extract

½ teaspoon salt

CARAMEL

1 cup butter

1 cup brown sugar

¼ cup corn syrup

1 can sweetened condensed
  milk (300 ml)

1 teaspoon vanilla

½ teaspoon salt

CHOCOLATE COATING

2 cups milk chocolate Callebaut callets,
  Chipits or chopped good quality
  chocolate from four 100-gram bars

SHORTBREAD CRUST

In the bowl of the stand mixer, cream together the butter and sugar until light and fluffy. Add in the flour, salt and vanilla and mix until combined. Press the crust evenly into the bottom of the prepared pan, being careful to press firmly into the corners and sides of the pan. Place the crust in the refrigerator for 30 minutes or in the freezer for 15 minutes.

Preheat the oven to 350°F. Place the crust in the oven and bake for 20 minutes, until the crust is golden brown. Set aside while you make the caramel. Note: If using a 9-inch square pan you will only need ¾ of the shortbread dough.

CARAMEL

In a medium heavy bottomed saucepan, melt the butter and add the sugar, corn syrup and condensed milk. Stir over medium heat and bring the mixture to a boil. Continue to cook at a low boil for 8 to 10 minutes. The mixture will become thick and tawny in color. The temperature of the caramel should read between 235°F to 240°F. Remove from heat and stir in the vanilla and salt. Pour the caramel over the crust and let cool at room temperature for 20 minutes, then refrigerate until cold.

FINISHING CHOCOLATE

In a heat proof bowl over a saucepan of simmering water, melt the chocolate. There should be no more than 2 inches of water in the saucepan. When the chocolate is melted and feels quite warm to the touch, remove from heat. The chocolate should be at a temperature of around 90°F.

If keeping the bars as pan squares, pour the chocolate over the cooled squares and let the chocolate set at room temperature for 2 hours or in the refrigerator for 30 minutes.

If making mini chocolate bars, place the bowl of chocolate on a tea towel next to the stove. Cut the bars into slim rectangles, approximately 4 inches by 1-inch. Using an elongated fork, dip each rectangle into the chocolate until it is fully enrobed in chocolate. With an offset spatula, remove any excess chocolate, before placing the rectangles on a parchment lined baking sheet. Before the chocolate is set, sprinkle the bars with sea salt.

These bars will keep in airtight containers in the refrigerator for one week or in the freezer for 2 months. It is best to wrap them in aluminum foil to keep the chocolate from discoloring.

Luscious Lemon Bars with Blackcurrant Jam

Preparation Time: 30 minutes / **Baking Time:** 20 minutes / **Chilling Time:** 30 minutes

Equipment: *Stand mixer or handheld mixer fitted with the paddle attachment, 13 x 9-inch baking pan lined with parchment paper.*

These lemon bars are complimented with a good quality blackcurrant jam. The blackcurrant jam is spread on top of a buttery shortbread crust and a tart lemon filling is poured on top, creating a perfect combination for a summery taste sensation, even in the dead of winter.

SHORTBREAD CRUST

1 cup butter

½ cup icing sugar

2 cups flour

1 teaspoon vanilla extract

½ teaspoon salt

1 cup blackcurrant jam for spreading over the baked pastry

LEMON FILLING

2 whole eggs and 4 egg yolks, at room temperature

1¼ cups sugar, divided

¼ cup flour

¾ cup lemon juice

1 tablespoon lemon zest

½ cup butter

Pinch of salt

SHORTBREAD CRUST

In the bowl of the stand mixer, cream together the butter and sugar until light and fluffy. Add in the flour, salt and vanilla and mix until combined. Press the crust evenly into the bottom of the prepared pan, being careful to press the crust firmly into the sides and corners. Place the crust in the refrigerator for 30 minutes or in the freezer for 15 minutes.

Preheat the oven to 350°F. Bake for 20 minutes, until the crust is golden brown. Let cool for 15 minutes before spreading the jam evenly over the crust. To prevent tearing the crust, warm the jam in the microwave and dollop the jam in about 7 places before spreading with an offset spatula. Refrigerate or freeze the jam filled crust until cold.

LEMON FILLING

Preheat the oven to 325°F. In a medium saucepan, melt the butter. Remove from the heat and whisk in 1 cup of sugar, the lemon juice and zest. In a small bowl, whisk the eggs and yolks together.

Combine the remaining sugar and flour well, then add to the eggs, whisking until the flour and sugar have been incorporated. Add the egg mixture to the saucepan whisking until smooth. Return the saucepan to the heat, stirring the lemon mixture over medium low heat until the curd begins to thicken to a custard-like consistency. Do not bring to a boil. Strain the mixture into a large measuring cup or pitcher. Pour carefully over the cold blackcurrant shortbread crust.

Bake the lemon bars for approximately 12 minutes. Let cool for 20 minutes at room temperature before refrigerating. Chill the lemon bars in the fridge for at least 2 hours or longer before slicing. Sift icing sugar over the cold bars for decoration.

These bars will keep in airtight containers in the refrigerator for 5 days or in the freezer for 1 month.

No Bake Cranberry Almond Date Bars

(GLUTEN-FREE, VEGAN)

Preparation Time: 25 minutes / **Chilling Time:** Overnight

Equipment: *One 9-inch square pan lined with parchment paper, food processor fitted with steel blade.*

Filled with fruit and nuts, this bar is good for a healthy energy snack or even for a breakfast on the go. I keep them individually wrapped in my freezer and grab one as needed. They are perfect lunch box additions.

2 cups dates

½ cup warmed apple juice

2 tablespoons brown sugar

½ cup unsweetened cranberries

¾ cup almonds, toasted

¾ cup quick oats, toasted

¼ teaspoon salt

½ cup natural or regular peanut butter

4 tablespoons cocoa powder

Preheat the oven to 350°F. Give the almonds a rough chop and spread the oats and almonds out on a parchment lined baking sheet and sprinkle with coarse sea salt. Bake for 8 minutes until the almonds and oats are fragrant and lightly browned. Set aside.

Place the dates in a heat proof bowl. Bring the apple juice to a simmer in a saucepan. Remove from the heat and pour over the dates, stirring the dates so that they are evenly covered in juice. Set aside for 10 minutes while the dates soften, stirring occasionally.

Drain the dates of any remaining liquid and place the softened dates in the bowl of the food processor. Add the sugar and pulse until the dates are of a thick paste consistency. Add the peanut butter (or tahini for a nut-free alternative), cocoa powder and salt. Pulse to combine. Next add the oats, almonds and cranberries and pulse briefly. You should now have a very thick, sticky mixture. Press the mixture into the prepared pan and place in the freezer overnight. Cut into bars and store in the refrigerator or freezer. These bars are best wrapped in aluminum foil and will keep in the refrigerator for one week and in the freezer for two months.

Layered Chocolate Almond Oatmeal Squares

Preparation Time: 20 minutes / **Baking Time:** 30 minutes

Equipment: *Stand mixer fitted with the paddle attachment or handheld mixer, one 13 x 9-inch baking pan lined with parchment paper and buttered.*

The chocolate in these bars is nicely balanced with the earthy flavor of the oats and the nutty flavor of the toasted almonds. They work well as an outdoor event snack, however, served warm with ice cream, they make a more than acceptable after dinner dessert.

1½ cups large flake quick rolled oats

1 cup toasted almonds, chopped.

1½ cups flour

1 teaspoon baking powder

1 teaspoon baking soda

½ teaspoon salt

1 cup packed brown sugar

½ cup white sugar

1 cup butter at room temperature

2 eggs at room temperature

2 teaspoons pure vanilla extract

2 cups dark 54% Callebaut chocolate callets or Chipits

1 cup milk chocolate Callebaut callets or Chipits

Preheat the oven to 350°F. Spread the almonds on a parchment lined baking sheet and toast for 5 to 7 minutes until golden brown and fragrant. Chop them fairly finely.

On a large sheet of parchment paper, whisk together the oats, almonds, flour, baking powder, baking soda and salt. In the bowl of the stand mixer, cream the butter and two sugars until light and fluffy. Add the eggs, one at a time, mixing after each addition. Add the vanilla extract. Tip in the dry ingredients and mix on low, occasionally scraping down the sides to the bottom of the bowl. With the mixer on low, add in the dark chocolate until just incorporated.

Spread half of the cookie dough onto the bottom of the prepared pan. Sprinkle one cup of milk chocolate callets or Chipits evenly over the dough, pressing them gently into the batter. Carefully, top with the remaining half of the dough.

Bake for 25 to 30 minutes or until the bars are golden brown. Let sit at room temperature for 20 minutes and then refrigerate for at least two hours, before slicing into squares or wedges. These bars will keep in airtight containers in the refrigerator for 1 week or in the freezer for 2 months.

Cakes

Banana Cake with Cream Cheese Icing, Caramel Drizzle & Maple Pecans

---

Preparation Time: 40 minutes / **Baking Time:** 45 to 50 minutes

---

Equipment: *Stand mixer fitted with the paddle attachment, or handheld mixer, one 9-inch round cake pan, buttered and floured and bottom lined with parchment paper, offset spatulas for spreading icing.*

This recipe is adapted from an Ina Garten recipe, called Old Fashioned Banana Cake. I have modernized it by adding salted caramel drizzle and maple pecans to the top of the cake. I also layered this cake and made it into a "naked" banana layer cake. However, it is wonderful as is, just one iced cake plain and simple to be enjoyed by you or your company with a nice cup of tea.

CAKE

3 very ripe bananas, cut into 1-inch pieces

¾ cup granulated sugar

½ cup brown sugar, lightly packed

½ cup vegetable oil

3 large eggs, room temperature

½ cup sour cream (generous)

1 teaspoon pure vanilla extract

Grated zest of 1 orange

2 cups flour

1 teaspoon baking soda

½ teaspoon salt

SALTED CARAMEL DRIZZLE

1 cup white sugar

¼ cup water

1 tablespoon corn syrup

¾ cup warmed whipping cream (place in microwave for 45 seconds)

2 tablespoons of butter

1 teaspoon vanilla extract

A pinch of salt

CREAM CHEESE FROSTING

2 blocks (500 grams) cream cheese, slightly cooler than room temperature

1 cup butter

1 teaspoon vanilla

4½ cups sifted icing sugar

MAPLE PECANS

1 cup pecans, lightly salted

½ cup maple syrup

CAKE

Preheat the oven to 350°F. Whisk together the flour, baking soda and salt on a large piece of parchment paper.

In the bowl of a stand mixer, mix the bananas, granulated sugar, and brown sugar on low speed until combined. Add the oil, eggs, sour cream, vanilla, and orange zest and beat on medium high speed until incorporated. With the mixer on low, tip in the dry ingredients and mix until just combined. Pour the batter into the prepared pan, smoothing the top with an offset spatula. Bake for approximately 45 to 50 minutes or until a toothpick comes out clean. The top of the cake will look quite brown. Cool the cake on a wire rack.

CARAMEL DRIZZLE

Place the sugar and the corn syrup in a medium sized saucepan. Pour the water evenly over the sugar being careful not to splash the sides of the pan. Shake the saucepan gently to even out the water over the sugar. Bring the sugar mixture to a boil over medium heat, stirring occasionally. Keep the syrup at a gentle boil until the sugar syrup turns into a medium dark amber color. Immediately remove the caramelized

Recipe continues on the next page

syrup from the heat. Place the whipping cream in the microwave for 45 seconds. Add the warmed whipping cream to the caramel, stirring constantly. It might boil up so be careful. Add the butter and stir until the butter is completely dissolved. Add salt to taste.

If the caramel is not completely smooth at this point you can return it to the heat and whisk until the proper texture is achieved. Chill in the fridge or freezer until the caramel is of slow pouring consistency.

MAPLE PECANS

Heat the maple syrup in a skillet until it reaches a slow boil. Add the pecans and stir the nuts until the maple syrup has crystallized around them. Scrape the nuts onto a parchment covered board and quickly separate them with an offset spatula.

CREAM CHEESE ICING

In the bowl of your stand mixer, beat the butter and cream cheese together until smooth. With the mixer on low, gradually add the icing sugar. Add 1 teaspoon vanilla and mix until smooth.

ASSEMBLY

Cut your cooled cake in half. Note: I use a serrated knife to cut the cake and insert toothpicks around the outside middle of the cake to serve as guides for my knife. This helps to achieve even layers. After slicing, refrigerate the cake layers for 1 hour. Place the bottom cake layer on a cutting board or cake board, cut side up. Generously frost the top of the layer, spreading the frosting right to the edges. Place the second layer on top, cut side up. With an offset spatula fill in any gaps in the icing between the layers.

Then, add more icing around the middle seam of the cake, and with an offset spatula, make a smooth band between the layers. Generously frost the top of the cake, making sure the top is evenly covered to the edges with frosting. Run the offset spatula around the top edge of the cake to give the icing definition.

Either pipe or drizzle the caramel with a spoon across the top of the cake, making crisscross lines. You can be as precise or rustic as you would like with this. To finish decorating, heap a small mound of maple pecans in the middle of the cake.

This cake will keep in the refrigerator for 5 days or can be frozen for up to 1 month. To freeze: place the cooled cake on a baking sheet in the freezer. When frozen, wrap in plastic wrap, then in aluminum foil.

Blood Orange Almond Tea Cake

(GLUTEN-FREE)

Preparation Time: 20 minutes / **Baking Time:** 35 minutes

Equipment: *A stand mixer with the whisk attachment, one 9-inch springform pan, buttered and lined with parchment paper.*

I love a flourless cake and the challenge it offers of preserving taste, rise and texture, all without gluten-free flour. Because of the almond flour and the addition of freshly squeezed orange juice, this cake is tender and moist. The best thing about it is that it keeps well at room temperature for at least 5 days. Adorned with a sprinkling of icing sugar and some chopped pistachios this cake can be served anywhere, at any time. However, it usually goes to my neighbors, who always appreciate a yummy, gluten-free dessert.

6 whole eggs at room temperature

1 cup white sugar

1 heaping tablespoon grated orange zest

1 teaspoon vanilla

¼ teaspoon almond extract

3 drops of pure orange extract

½ cup freshly squeezed orange juice from 2 blood oranges

2 tablespoons room temperature butter

2¼ cups almond flour

2 tablespoon icing sugar for dusting the top of the cooled cake

Preheat oven to 350°F. Simmer the orange juice in a small saucepan, until it has reduced to ⅓ cup. Take the juice off the heat and add 2 tablespoons of butter and stir until the butter is melted. Allow the mixture to cool to a lukewarm temperature. Place the eggs in the bowl of the stand mixer and whisk on medium speed until the mixture begins to thicken. Gradually add the sugar. Continue beating until the egg mixture doubles in volume and is thick enough that the whisk, when lifted, leaves a trail in the batter for 3 seconds. This will take at least 4 to 5 minutes. Note: This is an important step as the volume of the beaten eggs is the only way you can achieve lift in the cake. Add the extracts and orange zest.

With the stand mixer on low speed, add the almond flour until just incorporated. Still on low speed, stream in the orange juice and butter mixture until just combined. Empty the cake batter

Recipe continues on the next page

into the prepared springform pan. Bake for 35 to 40 minutes or until a toothpick inserted in the center comes out clean. Let cool on a wire rack.

Sift icing sugar over the top of the cake and garnish with chopped pistachios or toasted almonds. This cake stays fresh and moist for a good week, even on the counter. It can be frozen for up to 1 month. To freeze: place in the freezer on a baking sheet, unwrapped. When frozen, cover with plastic wrap, then with aluminum foil.

This neighborly cake is lovely served with creme fraiche. See creme fraiche recipe (page 253).

Wild Blueberry Jelly Roll

Preparation Time: 30 minutes / **Baking Time:** 15 minutes

Equipment: *A stand mixer fitted with a whisk attachment, or handheld mixer, a 12 x 18-inch or 11 x 15 jelly roll pan lined with parchment paper and greased.*

This is my sister Maureen's favorite recipe and she has been making this jam jelly roll, otherwise known as a Swiss roll, as a lunch dessert for years. The cake is light and pairs well with any good fruit jam. When I can get my hands on wild blueberries, bursting with fragrant flavor, this is one of my favorite desserts to make.

7 eggs, separated at room temperature

1 cup sugar, divided (4 tablespoons to be removed to be beaten with the egg whites)

¼ teaspoon cream of tartar

¼ teaspoon salt

2 teaspoons vanilla extract

1 cup cake flour, spooned, leveled, and sifted

½ teaspoon baking powder

¼ cup butter

1 jar of good quality jam

Place a clean tea towel sprinkled with icing sugar on a kitchen counter or table. This is where you will turn out your baked cake.

Preheat the oven to 375°F. In the bowl of the stand mixer, whisk the egg whites. When frothy, add the cream of tartar and salt. With the mixer on medium high speed, gradually begin to add the 4 tablespoons of sugar. Continue beating on high until soft peaks begin to form. Add the vanilla and beat until stiff peaks form. Remove the egg whites to a fresh bowl. Give the whisk and stand mixer bowl a quick wipe, place the yolks in the stand mixer bowl and begin to beat on medium high speed. When the yolks start to thicken, gradually add the rest of the sugar. Continue beating on high until the yolks have doubled in volume and are pale in color. A whisk run through the yolks should leave a trail. Take the bowl off the stand mixer. Sift together the flour and baking powder onto a piece of parchment paper. Tip half of the flour into the yolks, incorporating the flour with a hand whisk. Next fold in half the egg whites. Repeat with the remaining flour and egg whites, whisking until evenly incorporated.

Recipe continues on the next page

Next, place the butter in a medium-size microwave safe dish and microwave for 25 seconds, just until the butter is melted. It should be barely warm. Finally, take ½ cup of batter from the stand mixer bowl and combine it well with the butter. Add the butter/batter mixture back into the rest of the batter, stirring until the butter is well incorporated. Scrape the batter into the prepared jelly roll pan, smoothing the top and sides to the corners with an offset spatula. Tap on the counter to release any bubbles. Bake for 15 to 20 minutes. The top should be golden brown, and the cake should be just starting to pull away from the sides. Let the cake cool for approximately 4 minutes before loosening the sides with a sharp knife.

Tip the cake out onto the prepared tea towel and carefully remove the parchment paper from the back. Sprinkle the top of the cake with icing sugar. While still warm, but not hot, roll the cake up in the tea towel. Allow the cake to fully cool rolled up in the towel. When cool, unwrap the cake and spread the jam evenly over the cake leaving a small margin around the edges. Immediately roll up the cake and dust with icing sugar. Wrap in plastic wrap and refrigerate the rolled cake for at least two hours before slicing. You can dust the top of the cake once more with icing sugar, before serving.

This cake will keep in the refrigerator for 3 days or can be frozen for up to 1 month. To freeze: place the unwrapped cake on a baking sheet in the freezer. When frozen, wrap in plastic wrap, then in aluminum foil.

One Bowl Decadent Chocolate Cake Done 3 Ways

Preparation Time: 15 minutes / **Baking Time:** 25 minutes

Equipment: *Two 9-inch round cake pans buttered and lined with parchment paper, a large mixing bowl, a large measuring cup or pouring jug, a stand mixer fitted with the paddle attachment or handheld mixer. Note: You can also make the basic cake recipe in a 9 x 13 inch pan.*

This definitely is a go to cake for me, and while I risk jinxing myself, it seems to be a no fail recipe. The best thing about this cake is that it can all be done in one bowl! I have made it countless times for birthdays, work parties, showers, and barbeques much to everyone's delight. The basic cake recipe always remains the same, however, I do change up the frostings and the garnishes. For the Raspberry Version, I add a seedless raspberry jam to the layers and garnish the top with fresh raspberries. I frost this version with a silky chocolate buttercream. For the Mirror Glaze version, I frost the basic cake with a thin layer of the silky chocolate buttercream, skip the fruit, and pour a chocolate mirror glaze over the top of the cake. This results in a glossy, elegant finish. For the Ganache Version, I simply change out the buttercream on the top of the cake for ganache and garnish the cake with chocolate ganache filled raspberries.

THE BASIC CHOCOLATE LAYER CAKE
(for All Versions)

2 cups flour

1¾ cups sugar

¾ cup unsweetened cocoa powder

2 teaspoons baking soda

½ teaspoon salt

1 cup brewed coffee (for younger children you can use water)

¾ cup full fat buttermilk (I use Harmony)

¾ cup vegetable oil

1 teaspoon vanilla extract

3 large eggs at room temperature

BASIC CAKE

Preheat the oven to 350°F.

Sift the flour, sugar, cocoa powder, baking soda and salt into a large bowl and whisk the dry ingredients together. Form a well in the center. Combine the coffee, or water, buttermilk, vegetable oil, vanilla and eggs in a large measuring cup or jug. Stir until well combined. Pour this mixture into the well of the dry ingredients and whisk by hand until the wet ingredients are completely incorporated. Divide the cake batter between the two pans. Smooth the tops with an offset spatula. Bake the cakes for 25 minutes or until a cake tester comes out clean. If the cake layers form domes, place a clean tea towel on top of the cakes while still warm and gently press down to level the layers. Cool for 15 minutes in the pans. Then, remove the cakes from the pans and let them finish cooling on a cake rack.

Recipes continue on the following pages

Raspberry Chocolate Cake with Chocolate Buttercream

1 Basic Chocolate Layer Cake recipe (page 109)

1 cup of good quality seedless raspberry jam

1 tablespoon Chambord Raspberry liqueur (optional)

CHOCOLATE BUTTERCREAM FROSTING

1¼ cups butter

4 cups icing sugar

½ cup unsweetened cocoa powder

1 generous teaspoon pure vanilla extract

¼ teaspoon salt

½ cup whipping cream

GARNISH

2 pints of raspberries

1 teaspoon vanilla extract

3 large eggs at room temperature

RASPBERRY JAM FOR THE LAYERS

Warm 1 cup of seedless raspberry jam in the microwave for 35 seconds. Add the Chambord liqueur, if using, and stir. Reserve about ¼ cup of the warmed raspberry jam for the raspberry garnish on the top of the cake. While the cakes are still warm, take a toothpick or fork and prick all over the top of each cake layer. With a pastry brush, gently spread the top of each layer with the warmed raspberry jam.

CHOCOLATE BUTTERCREAM FROSTING

Sift the cocoa over the icing sugar on a large piece of parchment paper.

In the bowl of a stand mixer, cream the butter. Gradually tip in the icing sugar and cocoa until well incorporated. If the mixture is too thick at this stage, you can add some of the cream. Add the vanilla to the rest of the whipping cream and with the mixer on low-speed stream in the whipping cream. Change the speed to high and beat the frosting until smooth and velvety (approximately 2 minutes).

ASSEMBLY

Place the first cake layer jam side up on a working board or cake round. Spread the frosting evenly over the layer. Stack the second layer on top, with jam side up. Continue to frost the top and sides of the cake with the buttercream. Decorate the top with fresh raspberries. Dip a pastry brush into the reserved jam (it may need to be warmed up again) and brush the jam over the berries. This cake will keep in the refrigerator for 5 days or in the freezer for 1 month. To freeze: place the cooled cake unwrapped on a baking sheet in the freezer. When frozen, wrap in plastic wrap, then in aluminum foil. When ready to serve, thaw in the fridge, uncovered.

Mirror Glazed Chocolate Cake

Preparation Time: Cake: 25 minutes / Mirror Glaze: 25 minutes

Equipment: *1 medium heavy bottomed saucepan, a digital read thermometer (optional).*

A mirror glaze looks very elegant on a chocolate cake, especially if you garnish the top with fresh flowers. It is a little more difficult to accomplish than regular frosting as to achieve perfection the glaze has to be poured over the top of the cake in one go. However, I have made lots of mistakes doing this and with a little help from an offset spatula, dipped in hot water, no one has ever noticed the blemishes. This recipe involves covering the cake with a thin layer of the same chocolate buttercream used in Version 1, filling in any gaps between the layers, before you pour over the mirror glaze.

1 Basic Chocolate Layer Cake (page 109) and 1 Chocolate Buttercream Frosting (page 110)

MIRROR GLAZE

⅔ cup water

⅔ cup cream

1 cup plus 2 tablespoons of sugar

½ cup unsweetened cocoa powder

1 package of gelatin (2½ teaspoons) dissolved in 2 tablespoons of water

Frost the top of the first layer of cake generously, bringing the icing right to the edges. Top with the second layer, flat side up. Apply a thin layer of frosting over the top and sides of the cake, making sure to fill in any gaps between the layers. In order to ensure a smooth mirror glaze, place the frosted cake in the refrigerator for at least one hour, before glazing.

MIRROR GLAZE

Combine the water, cream, and sugar in a medium saucepan. Sift in the cocoa powder. Heat over medium heat, whisking constantly until the mixture is smooth. Continue to simmer for approximately 15 minutes until the mixture begins to thicken. Remove from heat. Pour 2 tablespoons of water into a small bowl and sprinkle over the gelatin. Stir to make sure the gelatin is completely dissolved. Allow the gelatin to bloom for 5 minutes. Add the gelatin to the warm chocolate glaze, stirring well to make sure the gelatin is fully incorporated. Allow the glaze to cool to approximately 80°F to 85°F, whisking as it cools. You can use a digital thermometer to check the temperature of the glaze or use your touch. It should feel warm, like a hot day.

Remove the cake from the fridge and place it on a wire rack set over parchment paper.

Pour the glaze from the saucepan into a good pouring jug or measuring cup. Stir gently to remove any large bubbles in the glaze. Have one or two offset spatulas at the ready.

Starting at the center of the cake, pour the glaze in a circular motion evenly over the top of the cake towards the outside, allowing the glaze to fall around the sides of the cake. If the glaze does not completely cover the sides of the cake, you can use an offset spatula and pour some more glaze to smooth it out. If bubbles form at the top of the cake, you can use a toothpick to break them.

This cake is best served on the same day. You can refrigerate or freeze it, however, you should allow it to come to room temperature for at least 5 hours to bring back the shiny look of the glaze, before serving.

Chocolate Ganache Cake

Preparation Time for Ganache: 15 minutes / **Chilling Time:** 1 hour

---

Equipment: *A stand mixer fitted with the whisk attachment, a heavy bottomed medium saucepan.*

Many people consider working with chocolate ganache easier than working with any other kind of frosting. Ganache mainly consists of two ingredients, whipping cream and chopped chocolate or chocolate in chip/callet form. You can pour a lukewarm ganache over a cake for a lovely finish. You can also whisk cooled ganache in a stand mixer or by hand to obtain a thicker, luscious, and lighter colored frosting. This recipe calls for using both methods to frost the cake. It is absolutely delicious and, like Version 1, is topped with fresh raspberries. However, for this cake, I do fill some of the raspberries with chocolate ganache. How decadent is that?!

1 Basic Chocolate Layer Cake
  (page 109)

CHOCOLATE GANACHE

3 cups Callebaut 54% dark
  chocolate callets, Chipits,
  or chopped 70% semi-
  sweet, good quality
  chocolate (approximately
  5 100-gram bars)
2 cups whipping cream

GARNISH

2 pints of fresh raspberries
2 tablespoons whipped
  ganache

Make the ganache. Place the chopped chocolate in a heat proof bowl. Pour the cream into a saucepan and bring to a simmer, just under a boil. Pour the hot cream over the chocolate, wait for 30 seconds, and then stir until smooth. Pour ⅓ of the ganache into a separate bowl and place in the refrigerator to cool. (This will become the whipped frosting for your middle layer.) Set aside the remaining saucepan of ganache on the counter and allow it to come to a lukewarm temperature. Stir the refrigerated ganache occasionally as it cools. You want the chocolate in the refrigerator to thicken, but you do not want the chocolate to harden. This will take about 30 minutes.

Place the cooled refrigerated ganache in the bowl of the stand mixer fitted with the whisk attachment. Whip the ganache until it becomes creamy and light in color. Add a pinch of salt to taste. Reserve 2 tablespoons of the whipped ganache to pipe into the raspberries for garnish.

ASSEMBLY

Place one of the cake layers flat side up on a cake board or counter and cover generously with the whipped ganache. Top with the second cake layer, flat side down and
fill in any gaps between the layers with the whipped ganache.

Pour the saucepan of ganache evenly over the top and down the sides of the cake.
You can smooth out the poured ganache with an offset spatula. Fill some raspberries
with the remaining whipped ganache (I use a piping bag with a small opening at the
tip to do this) and place them decoratively on top of the cake.

This cake keeps well in the refrigerator for 5 days and can be frozen without the
garnish for up to 1 month. To freeze: place the cooled cake unwrapped on a cookie
sheet in the freezer. When frozen, wrap in plastic wrap, then in aluminum foil.

Engaging Lemon Layer Cake
with Lemon Curd Filling

Preparation Time: 1 hour / **Baking Time:** 35 minutes

Equipment: *Stand mixer fitted with the paddle attachment or handheld mixer, two 8 or 9-inch cake pans, buttered and lined with parchment rounds.*

This elegant cake is perfect for any celebration and I have made it for countless engagement parties. It is a lemon lover's dream with a subtle lemon flavor in the cake combined with a tart lemon curd filling and a tangy lemon icing. You can make the lemon curd up to 3 days in advance and store it in the fridge for easy assembly. I have made this recipe into a three layer "naked" cake; however, it works equally well as a two-layer cake.

CAKE

¾ cup butter at room temperature

¼ cup vegetable oil

4 large eggs plus 2 yolks at room
   temperature

3 cups cake flour, spooned, leveled,
   and sifted

2 teaspoons baking powder

½ teaspoon baking soda

½ teaspoon salt

1¾ cups sugar

2 tablespoons lemon zest

2 teaspoons vanilla

1¼ cups buttermilk at room
   temperature

LEMON CURD

8 egg yolks

1¼ cups sugar

⅔ cup freshly squeezed lemon juice

1 tablespoon of lemon zest

½ cup butter

Pinch of salt

LEMON BUTTERCREAM

1¼ cups butter

4 cups icing sugar

1 teaspoon vanilla extract

2 tablespoons fresh lemon juice

¼ teaspoon salt

¼ cup whipping cream

LEMON CURD

Whisk the egg yolks together in a medium size saucepan. Add the sugar to the whisked yolks. Warm the lemon juice in the microwave for 40 seconds. It should be warm but not hot. Add the warm lemon juice to the egg yolk mixture gradually, whisking to combine. Add the zest and the salt. Note: The lemon curd can be made up to three days in advance.

Place the saucepan on medium low heat, whisking constantly, until the lemon mixture begins to simmer and thicken. This will take approximately 7 minutes. Do not boil the lemon curd or the eggs will curdle. The curd should be thick enough that it coats the back of a wooden spoon and when you run a finger across it, it leaves a trail. Take the curd of the heat and add the butter stirring until well incorporated. Sieve the curd into a non-reactive container. Let the steam evaporate from the hot curd, stirring the curd occasionally. Then cover the curd with plastic wrap, placing the wrap directly on the curd and chill in the refrigerator for at least 4 hours. If using on the same day, place the curd in the freezer.

CAKE

Preheat the oven to 350°F. Sift together the flour, salt, baking soda and baking powder on a large sheet of parchment paper. In a bowl, add the lemon zest to the sugar and stir until well combined and the sugar is moist and fragrant with lemon. In the bowl of the stand mixer, cream the butter and vegetable oil together until well incorporated. Gradually add the sugar and continue beating until light and fluffy. Add in the eggs and yolks one at a time, beating well after each addition. Add in the vanilla extract.

With the mixer on low, add the flour and buttermilk in three additions, beginning and ending with flour. Stop mixing when the flour is fully incorporated. Divide the batter evenly between the two prepared cake pans. Smooth the tops with an offset spatula and tap the pans on the counter to let out any air. Bake for 30 to 35 minutes or until a toothpick inserted into the center comes out clean. Let cool for 10 minutes before inverting onto a cake rack to cool completely.

LEMON BUTTERCREAM

In the bowl of a stand mixer, cream the butter with the icing sugar until smooth.

Add the vanilla and lemon juice and with the mixer on low, stream in the whipping cream. Beat the buttercream on high speed for approximately 2 minutes or until the icing is velvety and light.

Recipe continues on page 119

ASSEMBLY

Cut the two cakes in half. You will have 4 cake layers but will only need 3 layers to make this cake. Pick your best 3 layers and save the last layer for snacking, or to use in case of an emergency fix up during assembly. Note: To make even layers, I insert toothpicks around the middle of each cake to serve as guides. With a long serrated knife, I gently cut the layers with a back and forth motion, positioning the knife lightly on top of the toothpicks. Place one of the cooled cake layers on a cake board, placing a dab of icing in the middle of the cake board to secure the cake. Using a piping bag filled with icing, make a thin dam around the cake layer, and then fill the layer with the cold lemon curd. Place the second layer of the cake on top of the lemon curd filled layer. Once again, make a thin dam around this cake layer and then fill with lemon curd. Top with the 3rd cake layer, which will not be filled with lemon curd. Fill in any gaps between the layers with the icing and then make smooth bands of icing around the outside of each of the seams. Next, spread the icing evenly on the top layer of the cake, making it as smooth as possible.

Garnish the top of the cake with fresh flowers, twists of lemon peel, and/or some shaved white chocolate. This cake will keep in the refrigerator for up to 4 days or can be frozen for up to 1 month. To freeze: place the cake unwrapped on a baking sheet. When frozen, wrap well in plastic wrap, then in aluminum foil. Garnish on the day of serving.

Chocolate Peanut Butter Cake with Chocolate Peanut Butter Icing

Preparation Time: 20 minutes / **Baking Time:** 45 to 55 minutes

Equipment: *An 8 to 12 cup tube or Bundt pan, greased and floured, a stand mixer fitted with the paddle attachment or handheld mixer.*

You would think with the combination of peanut butter and chocolate that this cake would be almost too rich (if there is such a thing). However, the cake is surprisingly light in texture, while maintaining a beautiful depth of flavor. The topping is silky smooth and enhances the peanut butter and chocolate notes in the cake. It is by far one of the best cakes I make and has been sampled by many friends, family, and colleagues.

CAKE

1 cup dark 54% Callebaut chocolate callets, or Chipits, or chopped chocolate

1 cup conventional smooth peanut butter (I used Kraft)

1 cup butter at room temperature

1 cup white sugar

1 cup dark brown sugar

6 eggs

2 teaspoons pure vanilla extract

2¼ cups flour

2½ teaspoons baking powder

½ teaspoon salt

¾ cup milk

CHOCOLATE PEANUT BUTTER ICING

4 tablespoons butter

4 tablespoons peanut butter

4 tablespoons corn syrup

1½ cups dark 54% Callebaut chocolate callets or Chipits or chopped chocolate

2 tablespoons hot water

CAKE

Preheat oven to 350°F. Melt the chocolate in a heat proof bowl over a saucepan of simmering water. There should be no more than 2 inches of water in the saucepan. Stir until smooth, then set aside to cool.

On a large sheet of parchment paper, whisk together the flour, baking powder and salt.

In the bowl of the stand mixer, cream together the butter, peanut butter, and sugars until light and creamy. Add the eggs one at a time, beating well after each addition. Tip in the dry ingredients, alternately with the milk, until the flour is just blended. Pour half the batter into a separate bowl. Stir the chocolate into one of the bowls, until well mixed.

Using a spatula, empty the chocolate batter into the prepared pan. Cover with the peanut butter batter and using a knife, swirl the peanut butter batter into the chocolate batter.

Bake for 45 to 55 minutes or until the top springs back when touched and a skewer comes out clean.

CHOCOLATE PEANUT BUTTER ICING

Combine the chocolate, peanut butter, butter, corn syrup and hot water in a medium pan. Heat gently over the stove until the ingredients are blended and the chocolate peanut butter glaze is smooth. Spoon generously over the cooled cake.

This cake can be refrigerated for 5 days or can be frozen, iced, for 1 month. To freeze: place the cake unwrapped on a baking sheet and place in the freezer. When frozen, wrap in plastic wrap, then in aluminum foil.

Old Fashioned Sour Cream Donut Cake

Preparation Time: 20 minutes / **Baking Time:** 45 to 55 minutes

Equipment: *Stand mixer fitted with the paddle attachment, or handheld mixer, one 8 to 12 cup Bundt pan, sprayed with nonstick cooking spray or buttered and floured well.*

This cake tastes exactly like a cross between a sour cream and old-fashioned donut. It is the addition of oat flour to the recipe that helps give the cake its signature donut like texture and taste. A slice of this cake goes perfectly with a cup of coffee or tea. This is a great cake to take to work to liven up a coffee break.

1 cup butter at room temperature

1½ cups sugar

4 large eggs at room temperature

2 teaspoons pure vanilla extract

1½ cups buttermilk at room temperature

1 cup oat flour

2½ cups all-purpose flour

2 teaspoons baking powder

½ teaspoon baking soda

1 teaspoon salt

¼ teaspoon (generous) freshly ground nutmeg or powdered nutmeg

¾ teaspoon freshly grated cinnamon or powdered cinnamon

GLAZE

½ cup milk

3 cups icing sugar

½ teaspoon vanilla extract

Preheat the oven to 350°F. On a large piece of parchment paper, whisk together the two flours, baking soda, baking powder, salt, nutmeg, and cinnamon.

In the bowl of a stand mixer, cream the butter and sugar together until light and fluffy. Add the eggs one at a time, mixing thoroughly after each addition. Add the vanilla. With the mixer on low, tip in the dry ingredients alternately with the buttermilk, in three additions, beginning and ending with flour.

Pour the batter into the prepared Bundt pan making sure that the top is level, and the batter is smoothed to the edges. Give the pan a tap on the counter to release any air bubbles.

Bake in the preheated oven for 45 to 55 minutes or until a toothpick comes out clean.

Let the cake cool in the Bundt pan for 15 minutes. After 15 minutes, release the cake and let the cake cool completely on a wire rack.

GLAZE

In a small saucepan, warm the milk and vanilla and add the icing sugar until you have a paste-like consistency.

ASSEMBLY

While the cake still is warm, liberally apply the glaze to the top of the cake. Note: The top of the cake will be the top of the cake while baking, not the inverted top of the cake. You want the rougher side so that the cake mimics a doughnut. You can poke holes in the top of the cake with a toothpick if you want the glaze to really permeate the cake. Keep applying the glaze until the top of the cake is uniformly coated and the glaze is dripping down the sides.

Vanilla Cupcakes with Raspberry Buttercream

Preparation Time: 20 minutes / **Baking Time:** 23 minutes

Equipment: *A stand mixer fitted with a paddle attachment, 2 regular sized muffin trays, 24 cupcake liners.*

These cupcakes are light and fluffy and perfect for birthday parties, summer barbecues and school events. They are delightful when topped with fresh raspberries in season. This recipe makes 24 cupcakes, but you can easily halve the recipe.

CUPCAKES

2½ cups all-purpose flour

½ teaspoon salt

2 teaspoons baking powder

½ teaspoon baking soda

¾ cup butter at room temperature (quite soft is best)

¼ cup vegetable oil

4 large eggs at room temperature

1¾ cups sugar

1 tablespoon vanilla extract

1 cup buttermilk at room temperature

RASPBERRY BUTTERCREAM

1¼ cups butter at room temperature

4 cups of icing sugar

2 teaspoons of vanilla extract

½ cup of good quality raspberry jam

1 to 2 tablespoons of whipping cream or milk

CUPCAKES

Preheat the oven to 350°F. Whisk together the flour, salt, baking powder and baking soda on a large sheet of parchment paper. In the bowl of the stand mixer, fitted with the paddle attachment, cream together the butter, vegetable oil and sugar on medium high speed, until light and fluffy. Add the eggs one at a time, beating well after each addition. Add the vanilla. Tip in the flour mixture and mix on low speed until just incorporated. With a large cookie scoop, or pouring from a pitcher, fill the cupcake liners ¾ full. Bake for 20 to 25 minutes or until a toothpick inserted into the middle of a cupcake comes out clean.

RASPBERRY BUTTERCREAM

In the bowl of the stand mixer, cream the butter and icing sugar together. Add the jam and the vanilla. If the icing is too thick, add one or two tablespoons of whipping cream. Pipe or dollop the icing on the cupcakes. Garnish with fresh raspberries.

These cupcakes will keep in the fridge for up to 4 days or can be frozen, without garnish, in an airtight container in the freezer for up to 1 month.

Simple Carrot Cake Made Glorious

Preparation Time: 20 minutes / **Baking Time:** 45 to 50 minutes

Equipment: Two 9-inch cake pans, lined with parchment and buttered, a stand mixer fitted with the paddle attachment or handheld mixer.

Somehow you just can feel good about eating carrot cake, after all it does contain a vegetable rich in Vitamin A, K and C. My mother used to say: "Eat your carrots, it will help you see at night" and I keep this in mind every time I enjoy a piece or two. This carrot cake is loaded with fresh carrots, raisins soaked in orange juice and rum (optional) and fresh ripe pineapple. Canned pineapple can be substituted for fresh if a ripe pineapple is difficult to find. The entire cake is covered in cream cheese frosting. To make it even more special, I dipped cape gooseberries in caramel and set them on top of the cake. With their wispy outer wings, they lend a magical note to this dessert.

CAKE

2½ cups all-purpose flour scooped and leveled

½ teaspoon salt

1 tablespoon baking powder

1 teaspoon baking soda

2 teaspoons cinnamon

1 teaspoon ginger

¼ teaspoon nutmeg

¼ teaspoon allspice

1 cup chopped fresh ripe pineapple or canned pineapple

1¼ cups raisins soaked in 2 tablespoons orange juice and 3 tablespoons dark rum (rum optional)

2½ cups carrots (peeled, grated, and blotted on a paper towel)

1 cup brown sugar

¾ cup white sugar

1 cup vegetable oil (I use Canola)

4 large eggs at room temperature

FROSTING

3 blocks of cream cheese, 750 grams in total (slightly cooler than room temperature)

¾ cup butter at room temperature

4 cups icing sugar

2 teaspoons vanilla extract

CAKE

Preheat the oven to 350°F. Place the raisins, orange juice and rum, if using, in a small saucepan and warm over medium low heat for 2 or 3 minutes. Set aside to allow the fruit to soak up the spirits. Peel and grate the carrots (you will need 1 medium to large bunch of carrots) and blot on a paper towel. Chop up the fresh pineapple in ¼ inch pieces. If using canned pineapple, drain well and chop into ¼ inch pieces.

Whisk together the flour, salt, spices, baking powder and baking soda on a large sheet of parchment paper. In the bowl of the stand mixer, cream together the oil and sugar until light and fluffy. Add the eggs, one at a time, beating after each addition. With the mixer on low, tip in the dry ingredients and mix, until just blended. Add the raisins with any remaining liquid, the pineapple and the carrots and mix, until incorporated.

Divide the batter evenly between the prepared pans. Bake on the middle rack for 45 minutes or until a skewer inserted into the middle of the cake comes out clean. The tops of the cakes will look quite browned. Allow the cakes to cool for 15 minutes before turning them out onto a cake rack to cool completely.

FROSTING

In the bowl of the stand mixer, cream together the butter and cream cheese, until smooth. Add 2 teaspoons of vanilla extract. Gradually add the icing sugar, one cup at a time, until you reach the desired consistency.

GARNISH

I garnished this cake with Cape gooseberries and dipped the gooseberry fruit (not the leaves) into a caramel syrup. This was made by bringing 1 cup of sugar and ¼ cup of water to a boil and allowing the sugar to reach a rich amber color, before dipping the gooseberries.

ASSEMBLY

Place a dab of icing on a cardboard cake plate and center the first cake layer on the board. Spread the frosting evenly over the top of this cake layer before topping with your second cake layer. Generously cover the tops and sides of the cake, being careful to fill in any gaps between the layers. Place the gooseberries on top of the cake.

Vanilla, Vanilla Cake

Preparation Time: 30 minutes / **Baking Time:** 30 to 35 minutes

Equipment: *A stand mixer with the whisk attachment or handheld mixer, two 9-inch cake pans buttered and floured and lined with parchment paper.*

My favorite cake and by far the most difficult to make is a plain vanilla cake. I have probably experimented with over 100 recipes to obtain a cake that is finely crumbed, but not dry, moist but not leaden and has just the right amount of vanilla. Finally, I did it with this recipe by merging together the method and ingredients for a traditional yellow and white cake batter. This cake truly is versatile. It can be dressed up for an elegant evening event or dressed down for a casual get-together. The frosting on this cake is a vanilla buttercream made extra velvety with whipping cream.

CAKE

3 cups cake flour, lightly scooped, leveled and sifted

3 teaspoons of baking powder

½ teaspoon salt

¼ cup vegetable oil

¾ cup butter at room temperature. The butter should be quite soft in order to combine it with the vegetable oil, easily

4 whole eggs at room temperature

2 egg yolks at room temperature

2 cups sugar

1 tablespoon vanilla bean paste or extract

1¼ cups room temperature full fat buttermilk (I use Harmony)

VANILLA BUTTERCREAM FROSTING

1¼ cups butter at room temperature

4 cups icing sugar

2 teaspoons vanilla bean paste or extract

½ cup of whipping cream

Pinch of salt

Preheat the oven to 350°F. Sift the flour, baking powder and salt onto a large piece of parchment paper.

In the bowl of the stand mixer fitted with the whisk attachment, cream the butter and the vegetable oil together until they are well combined. Gradually add the sugar and beat on high speed until the mixture is light and fluffy. Add the eggs and yolk, one at a time, beating after each addition. Add the vanilla bean paste or extract.

With the mixer on low speed, tip the flour mixture into the egg mixture, alternating with the buttermilk, in 3 additions, beginning and ending with flour. Do not overmix the batter at this stage. Once each addition of flour and buttermilk has been absorbed, move on to the next addition. Pour the batter into the cake pans and smooth the tops with an offset spatula. Bake for approximately 30 to 35 minutes or until a toothpick inserted into the center comes out clean. Cool on a wire rack.

VANILLA BUTTERCREAM FROSTING

In the bowl of the stand mixer, cream the butter on medium speed. Gradually add the icing sugar until all the sugar has been incorporated. Add the vanilla to the whipping cream and stream the whipping cream into the icing. Once the cream has been fully incorporated, turn the speed of the mixer to high and continue to beat the frosting until it becomes smooth and velvety (about 2 minutes). Add a pinch of salt to taste.

ASSEMBLY

Place a dab of frosting on a cake board or plate and set the first layer of cake on the board. With an offset spatula, spread the frosting on the cake, being careful to maintain a uniform thickness and to go all the way to the sides. Cover with the top layer and fill in any gaps between the two layers with the frosting. Frost the top and the sides of the cake. Garnish with white chocolate shavings.

This cake can be refrigerated for 1 week or frozen for up to 1 month. Freeze the cake unwrapped on a cookie sheet. When frozen, wrap in plastic wrap, then in aluminum foil.

Cherry Pound Cake Loaf

Preparation Time: 20 minutes / **Baking Time:** 50 to 60 minutes

Equipment: *Two standard loaf pans buttered and lined with parchment paper, a stand mixer or handheld mixer fitted with the paddle attachment.*

My first real crush on a boy happened when I was in Grade 8. He sat beside me in science class, when we were dissecting frogs. Of course, he tried to freak me out by making the formaldehyde frogs legs dance on my arm, but he made up for it at lunch. He came over and shared a slice of his mother's cherry pound cake with me. I quickly moved on from my crush on this young man, but I never got over my infatuation with a good cherry pound cake.

1½ cups butter

2½ cups sugar

6 large eggs, room temperature

2 teaspoons pure vanilla extract

½ teaspoon almond extract

2 cans of Bing cherries, well drained and left to dry on paper towels (reserve the juice for icing)

1 cup sour cream

3 cups flour, scooped and leveled

2 teaspoons baking powder

½ teaspoon baking soda

½ teaspoon salt

GLAZE

¼ cup of reserved cherry juice

½ teaspoon vanilla

2 cups icing sugar

Preheat the oven to 350°F. On a large piece of parchment paper, whisk together the flour, baking soda, baking powder and salt.

In the bowl of the stand mixer, cream together the butter and sugar. Add the eggs, one at a time, beating well after each addition. Add the extracts. Tip in the dry ingredients and mix until just incorporated, scraping down to the bottom of the bowl with a spatula, occasionally. Add the sour cream and incorporate on a low speed. Lightly flour the drained cherries. Take the bowl off the stand and fold in the cherries by hand. Pour the batter into the prepared loaf pans.

Bake for 50 to 60 minutes or until a toothpick inserted in the center comes out clean. Let cool in the loaf pans for 20 minutes before inverting onto cake racks.

GLAZE

Whisk together the remaining cherry juice, icing sugar and vanilla. When the cake is cool, apply the glaze and lightly dust with icing sugar.

These loaves will keep in the refrigerator for 1 week and can be frozen for up to 1 month. To freeze: place unwrapped in the freezer on a baking sheet. Once frozen, cover with plastic wrap, then with aluminum foil.

Date & Nut Loaf

(GLUTEN-FREE, VEGAN)

Preparation Time: 25 minutes / **Baking Time:** 45 minutes

Equipment: *A 9 x 5-inch loaf pan, lined with parchment paper with an overhang of one inch, a food processor fitted with a steel blade.*

This is a dense, very flavorful date and nut loaf that can be served alone for breakfast or with an afternoon tea or coffee. It is a good recipe to have in your pocket when expecting vegan guests and makes for a lovely gift for friends who practice a gluten-free or vegan diet.

1½ cups dates, pitted and coarsely chopped

1 cup almond milk

2 tablespoons dark brown sugar

1 teaspoon vanilla extract

2 tablespoons Bob Red Mill's egg replacer mixed with 4 tablespoons water

⅓ cup vegetable oil (I used Canola)

2 teaspoons apple cider vinegar or lemon juice

¾ cup walnuts, toasted

1⅔ cups oat flour

⅓ cups almond flour

1 teaspoon baking powder

1 teaspoon baking soda

1 teaspoon cinnamon

½ teaspoon salt

¼ cup rolled oats for sprinkling on top of the loaf

Preheat the oven to 350°F. Sprinkle the walnuts with sea salt and bake on a parchment lined cookie sheet for 10 minutes until fragrant and browned. When cool, chop the walnuts into ¼ inch pieces. Place the dates in a medium sized mixing bowl. Bring the almond milk to a simmer in a saucepan. Remove from the heat and pour over the dates. Allow the dates to soften in the hot milk for 10 minutes stirring occasionally.

Mix the egg replacer with the water and allow to sit for one minute. Whisk together the two flours, baking powder, baking soda, cinnamon and salt together in a large bowl. In the bowl of the food processor, pulse the softened dates and any remaining milk, brown sugar, vegetable oil and apple cider vinegar until you have a thick paste. Add the egg replacer and pulse until just combined. Make a well in the bowl of dry ingredients and scrape the date mixture into the well. Add the walnuts and mix with a spoon or spatula until you have incorporated all the nuts into the batter.

Spoon the batter into the prepared pan. Sprinkle the oats on top of your loaf. Bake for 45 to 55 minutes or until a toothpick inserted into the center comes out clean. This loaf can be wrapped and refrigerated for 5 days or frozen for 1 month.

Pumpkin Loaf with Maple Glaze & Maple Pecans

(VEGAN)

Preparation Time: 20 minutes / **Baking Time:** 1 hour and 5 minutes

Equipment: *A 9 x 5 or 9 x 4-inch loaf pan lined with parchment paper, a large mixing bowl.*

The maple glaze and maple candied nuts harmonize well with the pumpkin flavor in this nicely spiced tender loaf. I have added just enough ginger to give the loaf a touch of warmth for enjoying on a cold crisp day. This is a nice loaf to bring to community gatherings as most everyone can enjoy it. It often makes an appearance at our annual Fall Community Street Party.

LOAF

1¾ cups flour

1½ teaspoons cinnamon

¾ teaspoon ginger

¼ teaspoon allspice

½ teaspoon baking powder

1 teaspoon baking soda

½ teaspoon salt

1 tablespoon flaxseed mixed with 2½ tablespoons water (This is your flaxseed egg)

15 ounces, 1½ cup pure pumpkin puree

1¼ cups brown sugar

½ cup Canola oil or any other vegetable oil

¼ cup almond milk

GLAZE

⅓ cup maple syrup

1½ cups icing sugar

A pinch of salt

Maple Pecans (see recipe under Banana Cake, page 100)

LOAF

Preheat the oven to 350°F. Combine the flaxseed with the water and let sit until the mixture thickens (about 15 minutes). In a large bowl combine the pumpkin puree, sugar, oil, almond milk, then the flaxseed. With a hand whisk, mix until the ingredients are well incorporated. On a large piece of parchment paper, whisk together the flour, spices, and salt. Add the dry ingredients to the wet ingredients and combine well. Pour the batter into the prepared pan, smoothing the top with an offset spatula. Bake for 1 hour and 5 minutes or until a toothpick inserted into the center comes out clean. Let the loaf cool in the pan for 20 minutes. Then release onto a cake rack to cool completely.

MAPLE GLAZE

In a small saucepan on medium low heat, combine the maple syrup and icing sugar. Continue whisking until there are no lumps and the glaze is of a nice pouring consistency. If the glaze needs to be thicker add more icing sugar. Remove from the heat and continue whisking for a few minutes as the glaze cools down in order to ensure a smooth consistency. Pour over the lukewarm cake in two additions. Garnish with the maple pecans.

Old Fashioned Biscuit Shortcakes with Peaches in Sauterne

Preparation Time: 25 minutes / **Chilling Time:** 30 minutes / **Baking Time:** 20 minutes

Equipment: *Two 12 x 18-inch cookie sheets, a food processor fitted with the steel blade, a stand mixer fitted with the whisk attachment or handheld mixer.*

This is an old-fashioned shortcake recipe made with lemon zested buttermilk biscuits, which simply crumble in your mouth, as you savor the taste of the fresh peaches and whipped cream. I used fresh peaches in season for this recipe, but canned cling peaches work almost as well. Just drain the peaches, before you marinate them in the sauterne. This recipe makes 8 to 10 shortcake biscuits.

Peaches in Sauterne
  (page 138)

BISCUITS

3 cups flour

⅓ cup sugar

3 teaspoons baking powder

1 teaspoon baking soda

½ teaspoon salt

1 cup cold butter cut
  into cubes

1¼ cups buttermilk

Grated zest of 1 lemon

Cream and sugar (for brushing
  and sprinkling on top of
  the biscuits)

WHIPPED CREAM

1½ cups whipping cream

⅓ cup sugar

½ teaspoon vanilla extract

PEACHES

Follow the instructions for Peaches in Sauterne on page 138.

BISCUITS

Place the flour, salt, sugar, zest, baking soda and baking powder into the bowl of the food processor. Pulse to combine. Add the cubes of butter and pulse in brief intervals, until the butter has dispersed into smaller pieces throughout the flour. Do not overmix.

Scrape the mixture from the food processor into a large mixing bowl. Make a well in the center of these ingredients and pour in the buttermilk. Stir with a wooden spoon until the buttermilk just is incorporated. Drop the batter by ⅓ cups onto the prepared baking sheets, 3 inches apart. I place 5 biscuits on each sheet. With floured hands, roughly shape the biscuits into tall rounds. Refrigerate the biscuits for 30 minutes to prevent spreading in the oven.

Preheat the oven to 400°F. Brush the biscuits with cream and/or milk and sprinkle with white or turbinado sugar. Bake for 20 minutes or until golden brown. Let cool on wire racks.

WHIPPED CREAM

In the bowl of a stand mixer or with a handheld mixer, beat the whipping cream, gradually adding the sugar as the cream thickens. Add the vanilla extract as soon as the cream forms soft peaks. Continue beating until stiff peaks form.

TO SERVE

Cut each biscuit in half. Fill with peaches and whipped cream. Top with the remaining half and garnish with more peaches and whipped cream. The biscuits can be frozen before being filled for up to 1 month. Simply place the cooled biscuits in airtight bags before freezing.

Burnt Basque Cheesecake Topped with Pineapple Flowers

Preparation Time: 20 minutes / **Baking Time:** 1 hour

Equipment: *A 10-inch springform pan, bottom double lined with parchment paper, a stand mixer fitted with the paddle attachment or handheld mixer.*

The latest trend in cheesecakes seems to be of the Spanish variety. Unlike American cheesecakes, these are crustless and cooked at a higher heat, which results in a wonderful, caramelized "burnt" top. I have added pineapple flowers to the top of the cake, which simply consist of very thin slices of pineapple baked in the oven at a low heat for a long time. They are beautiful to look at and sweet and crunchy to the taste. I have included a recipe below.

CHEESECAKE

4 blocks of cream cheese
   (1000 grams)
1½ cups sugar
6 large eggs, room temperature
2 teaspoons vanilla
½ teaspoon salt
1½ cups whipping cream
⅓ cup flour, sifted

PINEAPPLE FLOWERS

1 fresh pineapple, outer rind
   and brown spots removed

Preheat the oven to 400°F. In the bowl of the stand mixer, cream the cheese and gradually add the sugar until very smooth. With the mixer on low, add the eggs one at a time, beating well after each addition. Add the cream, salt and vanilla and beat until thoroughly combined. Sift the flour over the batter and mix on low speed until incorporated. Pour the batter into the prepared pan.

Bake the cheesecake until the top is a rich golden brown and the center has a slight jiggle. About 60 minutes. If you have a hot oven and the top starts to brown too early, you can tent the cheesecake with aluminum foil at the 45-minute mark. Allow to cool at room temperature for at least 2 hours before placing in the refrigerator to set up completely. The cheesecake is best left in the refrigerator overnight before serving.

PINEAPPLE FLOWER GARNISH

Preheat the oven to 225°F. Cut off the top end of the pineapple and remove the outer rind. With a potato peeler, remove any brown spots that are remaining. With a very sharp knife, slice the pineapple as thinly as you can. You also can use a mandolin for this. Blot the pineapple slices on a paper towel and place them on a parchment lined baking sheet. Bake for 2 hours. Remove the slices from the oven and either place the warm, dried pineapple slices in a muffin tin to shape them like flowers or allow them to dry flat. Note: This step can be done 3 days ahead of time.

This cheesecake will keep in the refrigerator for 5 days or can be frozen for up to 1 month. To freeze: place the cold cheesecake still in the pan on a baking sheet in the freezer. When frozen, remove the pan, cover in plastic wrap, then in aluminum foil.

Decadent Dark Chocolate Cheesecake with Chocolate Ganache

Preparation Time: 25 minutes / **Baking Time:** 1 hour

Equipment: *A 9 or 10-inch springform pan, buttered and lined with parchment paper, a stand mixer fitted with the paddle attachment or handheld mixer.*

This cake has a triple layer of chocolate from the Oreo crumb crust and the chocolate cheese filling to the smooth chocolate ganache topping. However, a small slice is all you need to satisfy your chocolate craving for the week. I usually serve this to a large group and make it well in advance. The cheesecake freezes beautifully, and I let it thaw in the refrigerator on the day I serve it. I often complement the chocolate ganache by topping the cake with some fresh raspberries or strawberries. If I am feeling decadent, I fill the strawberries with whipped cream. Did I say that this was a crowd pleaser?

COOKIE CRUST

- 1½ cups chocolate Oreo crumbs
- ½ cup almond flour
- ½ cup dark 54% Callebaut callets or Chipits
- ½ cup butter
- 2 tablespoons sugar
- ¼ teaspoon salt

CAKE

- 2 cups dark 54% Callebaut callets, Chipits or chopped chocolate (you will need four 100-gram bars)
- 4 bricks (250 grams each) of cream cheese
- 1 cup white sugar
- 2 tablespoons of unsweetened cocoa powder
- 4 large eggs at room temperature
- 2 teaspoons pure vanilla extract
- ¾ cup sour cream

CHOCOLATE GANACHE

- 2 cups dark 54% Callebaut callets, Chipits or chopped chocolate (approximately three 100-gram bars)
- 2 tablespoons butter
- 1 tablespoon corn syrup
- 1¼ cups whipping cream
- Pinch of salt

GARNISH

Fresh raspberries or strawberries filled with whipped cream (optional)

CRUST

Preheat the oven to 350°F. In a medium bowl, whisk together the chocolate crumbs, almond flour, salt, sugar, and chocolate. Melt the butter and combine well with the dry ingredients. The chocolate will melt a little which is fine. It helps to hold the crust together. Press into the bottom of the springform pan. Bake for 8 minutes and allow to cool in the refrigerator or freezer.

CAKE

Melt the chocolate in a heat proof bowl over a saucepan of simmering water, stirring constantly. The water should not exceed 2 inches. Set aside to cool. In the bowl of the stand mixer, beat the cream cheese, gradually adding the sugar. Add the eggs, one at a time, beating after each addition. Add the vanilla. With the mixer on low, add in the sour cream. Once the sour cream is incorporated, sift the cocoa powder into the cheese mixture and blend. Tip the cooled chocolate into the filling and mix until smooth.

Pour the filling into the cooled crust and bake for 1 hour. The sides should be set, and the middle should be mostly set, but can have a slight jiggle. Let the cheesecake cool in the pan at room temperature for at least 2 hours. Then refrigerate in the pan, until cold.

GANACHE

Place the chocolate in a heat proof bowl with the butter and corn syrup. Heat the whipping cream in a small saucepan until the cream comes to a simmer, just under a boil. Pour the hot cream over the chocolate, wait 30 seconds, then stir the chocolate until smooth. Note: If, after stirring, there are unmelted pieces of chocolate, you can just place the heatproof bowl over simmering water and keep stirring the mixture, until smooth. Set the ganache aside, stirring occasionally until the chocolate reaches a good pouring consistency. You can hasten this process by placing the ganache in the refrigerator, but you have to keep an eye on it as the chocolate can harden quickly.

Recipe continues on the next page

ASSEMBLY

With the cheesecake still in the pan, pour the ganache over the top of the cheesecake. Smooth to the edges with an offset spatula. If you would like to have the chocolate drip down the sides of the cheesecake, simply remove the cake from the pan and pour the ganache, in a circular motion, encouraging it to drip over the edges. Decorate with fresh raspberries or strawberries. I like to quarter the strawberries almost to the stem and then fill them with whipped cream.

This cake will keep in the refrigerator for up to 5 days and can be frozen for up to 1 month. To freeze: place the cold cheesecake still in the pan in the freezer. When frozen, remove the pan and cover with plastic wrap, then wrap in aluminum foil.

Coconut Cream Cake
with Chocolate Ganache

Preparation Time: 20 minutes / **Baking Time:** 55 to 60 minutes

Equipment: *One 8 to 12 cup Bundt or tube pan, buttered and floured, a stand mixer fitted with the whisk attachment or handheld mixer.*

This is a very moist cake and has a lovely coconut flavor, which comes from a full tin of coconut cream. I did not add shredded coconut to the batter as I wanted a smooth consistency. However, I did add lots of organic toasted coconut to the top of the cake. I always buy organic unsweetened coconut and then sweeten and toast the coconut myself. The flavor is indescribably better than the sweetened packages of coconut found in most grocery store aisles. The recipe for sweetening and toasting the coconut can be found below.

CAKE

¾ cup butter at room temperature

5 eggs at room temperature, separated

1 tin of coconut cream, not milk, or
    1½ cups

1¾ cups white sugar plus ¼ cup white
    sugar to whisk with the egg whites

2½ cups flour

2 teaspoons baking powder

½ teaspoon baking soda

½ teaspoon salt

2 teaspoons pure vanilla extract

1 teaspoon coconut extract
    (optional, the taste will still be
    of coconut without, but milder)

CHOCOLATE GANACHE

See recipe under Decadent Dark
    Chocolate Cheesecake,
    page 143

COCONUT GARNISH

2 cups of organic unsweetened
    coconut

½ cup water

½ cup sugar

2 teaspoons vanilla extract

Preheat the oven to 350°F. On a large sheet of parchment paper, whisk together the flour, baking powder, baking soda and salt. In the bowl of the stand mixer fitted with the whisk attachment beat the egg whites. When foamy, gradually add ¼ cup of sugar. Continue beating on high speed until the egg whites are glossy and form stiff peaks. Scrape the whites out into a fresh bowl. Give the bowl and whisk of the stand mixer a quick wipe.

Cream the butter and the remaining sugar together. Add the egg yolks one at a time, waiting until each yolk is fully incorporated, before adding the next. Tip in the dry ingredients, alternating with the coconut milk, in three additions, beginning and ending with the flour. Remove the bowl from the stand and carefully fold in the egg whites. Scrape the batter into the prepared pan, using an offset spatula to smooth the batter to the edges. Bake for 55 to 60 minutes, until the top springs back to the touch and a toothpick inserted into the center comes out clean. It is best to check the cake for doneness at the 50-minute mark. Let cool in the pan for 10 minutes, then invert onto a cake rack.

CHOCOLATE GANACHE

See instructions under Decadent Dark Chocolate Cheesecake (page 143).

COCONUT GARNISH

Preheat the oven to 350°F. Heat the water, sugar, and vanilla in a saucepan over medium heat, until the sugar is dissolved. Add the coconut and stir until all the coconut has been covered with the syrup. With a slotted spoon, spread the coconut out onto a parchment lined baking sheet. Bake for 7 to 8 minutes, stirring halfway in order to evenly toast the coconut. The coconut should be lightly browned. Set aside to cool. (This can be made a week ahead.)

ASSEMBLY

Pour the chocolate ganache liberally over the cake. The ganache can be lukewarm as it will set on the cake. If serving on the same day, sprinkle the toasted coconut over the ganache. If serving later, store the coconut in a Ziploc bag in the cupboard and add on the day of serving.

This cake will keep in the fridge for 5 days or can be frozen for up to 1 month. To freeze: place on a baking sheet in the freezer, unwrapped. When frozen, wrap in plastic wrap, then in aluminum foil.

Earthen Chocolate Cake

(GLUTEN-FREE)

Preparation Time: 20 minutes / **Baking Time:** 40 minutes

Equipment: *A stand mixer fitted with the whisk attachment or a handheld mixer, a 9-inch springform pan, lined with parchment and buttered.*

Many flourless chocolate cakes are thin and dense in texture, because of the amount of chocolate used and the absence of raising agents such as baking soda and powder. While this cake recipe uses 1 pound of chocolate, it calls for 8 eggs, separated. The yolks emulsify the chocolate mixture, and the beaten whites cause the cake to rise. Consequently, this is one of my favorite flourless chocolate cakes. It tastes both decadently rich in chocolate and light and creamy, at the same time. This is a perfect dinner party dessert, especially as it can be eaten by guests who are on a gluten-free diet.

1 pound (approximately 2¾ cups) dark 54% Callebaut callets or chopped 70% dark chocolate from five 100-gram bars (I recommend Lindt or Green and Black)

½ cup butter

¼ cup strong brewed coffee, warm.

8 large eggs separated, at room temperature

¾ cup sugar plus 2 tablespoons for whisking with the egg whites

2 teaspoons vanilla extract

½ teaspoon salt

Preheat the oven to 350°F. Melt the butter in a heavy bottomed saucepan or on the top of a double boiler. Add the chocolate and stir until combined and smooth. Add the brewed coffee and continue stirring until the coffee is completely incorporated. Set aside.

In the bowl of the stand mixer, whisk the egg whites on medium speed. When frothy and beginning to thicken, add ½ teaspoon salt and 2 tablespoons of sugar. Continue beating the egg whites until they form stiff peaks. Transfer the egg whites to a clean mixing bowl.

Wipe out the bowl of the mixer and the whisk and begin to work on the yolks. Place the yolks in the bowl of the mixer and whisk on medium speed. Once the yolks have begun to thicken, gradually add the rest of the sugar. Continue beating until the yolks are pale in color and doubled in volume (at least 3 minutes).

With the mixer on low speed, add ⅓ of the chocolate mixture to the yolks. When this is incorporated, add the rest of the chocolate, and continue to mix on low speed until just combined.

Remove the bowl from the stand mixer. Fold in ⅓ of the egg whites. Then fold in the rest of the egg whites making sure you scrape down to the bottom of the mixing bowl. Pour the batter into your prepared pan. Bake for approximately 40 minutes until the edges are cracked and the middle is just set. A skewer inserted into the middle of the cake should have a few moist crumbs clinging to it. Let stand for 10 minutes, then unmold. Decorate with icing sugar or fresh fruit.

This cake will keep in the refrigerator for 5 days or can be frozen for up to 1 month. To freeze: place in the freezer, unwrapped on a baking sheet. When frozen, cover in plastic wrap, then in aluminum foil.

Easy Chocolate Lava Cakes

Preparation Time: 20 minutes / **Baking Time:** 12 minutes

Equipment: *4 ramekins, buttered and floured, a stand mixer fitted with the whisk attachment, or handheld mixer.*

Originally created by Chef Jean-Georges Vongerichten, I would have to say that this is the easiest chocolate lava cake recipe I have ever made. This makes 4 rather full ramekins; however, you can double the recipe to make more. It is important to use good quality chocolate as the molten chocolate is the star of this dish. I used Lindt, but any good quality chocolate bar can be substituted. The lava cakes can be kept in the fridge for one day prior to baking which makes them a handy dessert to serve to your company. If making the cake ahead, bring the batter to room temperature prior to baking. These cakes take such a short time to bake that you can choose your moment, during dinner, to put them in the oven. Guests always are joyfully surprised to smell chocolate baking as they are finishing up their main course. Ice-cream and crème fraiche (see recipe on page 253) make stellar additions to this dessert.

½ cup butter

1 cup good quality 70% chocolate chopped (two 100-gram bars)

2 eggs, room temperature

2 yolks, room temperature

⅓ cup sugar

¼ teaspoon of salt

2 tablespoons flour

Preheat the oven to 425°F. Set the prepared ramekins on a baking sheet. In a saucepan over medium low heat, melt the butter and the chocolate, stirring all the while. Set aside. In the bowl of the stand mixer, beat the eggs, yolks, sugar, and salt until thickened and pale. Fold in the chocolate, then sift in the flour. Spoon the batter into the prepared ramekins and bake for 12 minutes. The sides should be firm, but the middle should look soft. Let the cakes cool for 1 minute before covering each with an inverted dessert plate. Carefully, turn each plate over. Alternatively, serve in the ramekin, wrapped in a pretty cloth napkin, to prevent the quests from burning themselves.

Mango Cakelets on Fire

Preparation Time: 45 minutes / **Baking Time:** 15 minutes

Equipment: *A stand mixer fitted with the whisk attachment or handheld mixer, a 12 x 18-inch jelly roll pan or rimmed cookie sheet, lined with parchment and buttered, a 3 to 4-inch round cookie cutter.*

Genoise cakes can be a bit tricky as you have to pay attention to how you mix the ingredients. If you overmix the batter, the cake will turn out rubbery. The eggs must be allowed to triple in volume and the flour and butter have to be gently incorporated. Although flavorful, this type of cake tends to be on the dry side. Consequently, a simple syrup often is added to the layers. For this recipe, I have used a simple orange brandy syrup. You can omit the brandy and just use fresh orange juice. Topped with fresh mango slices and filled with mango whipped cream, these individual cakes are truly beautiful to behold.

CAKE

6 room temperature eggs
¾ cup sugar, divided
1 cup cake flour, lightly scooped,
   then sifted
½ teaspoon baking powder
¼ teaspoon salt
⅓ cup butter melted with
   2 teaspoons vanilla

MANGO WHIPPED CREAM

4 ripe Ataulfo mangos
   (you will need 1 for garnish)
2 cups whipped cream
⅓ cup skim milk powder
½ cup icing sugar
1 teaspoon vanilla

SIMPLE SYRUP

¾ cup sugar
½ cup water
¼ cup orange juice
Peel from 1 orange
1 tablespoon brandy

SIMPLE ORANGE SYRUP

Heat the water, juice, sugar, vanilla, peel, and brandy, if using, in a small saucepan over medium high heat. Allow to boil for 4 minutes, then remove from the heat and set aside to cool.

CAKE

Preheat the oven to 350°F. Sift the cake flour, salt, and baking powder onto a piece of parchment paper.

Whisk the eggs in a heat proof bowl set over a saucepan of simmering water. There should be no more than 2 inches of water in the saucepan. Gradually add ½ cup sugar to the eggs and continue whisking until the sugar is dissolved and the egg mixture is warm to the touch. Remove from the heat and tip the egg mixture into the bowl of the stand mixer. Beat on medium high speed, adding the rest of the sugar gradually. Continue beating on high until the eggs have tripled in volume, become pale in color and a whisk moved through the eggs leaves a distinct trail.

While the eggs are being whisked, melt the butter in a cereal sized dish in the microwave for 30 seconds. Add the vanilla. Set aside.

Remove the bowl from the stand mixer and gently fold in the flour, one third at a time. Scrape right down to the bottom of the bowl. Many pastry chefs do this with their hands. Once the flour has been gently incorporated, remove 1 cup of batter and whisk it into the dish with the melted butter. Then, gently add this back into the rest of the batter in the stand mixer bowl.

Pour the cake batter onto the prepared baking sheet. Using an offset spatula, spread the batter evenly to the sides and ends of the sheet. Give the tray a quick bang on the counter to release any air bubbles. Bake for approximately 12 to 15 minutes. The cake should be a light golden color and spring back when touched. Allow to cool for 5 minutes and then tip the cake onto a clean piece of parchment paper, sprinkled with icing sugar. Gently, remove the parchment paper from the back of the cake. While still warm, brush the cake all over with the orange syrup.

MANGO WHIPPED CREAM

Cut three of the mangos into smallish ¼ inch pieces. Reserve one mango to be sliced thinly for garnish. Place the whipping cream in the bowl of the stand mixer and add the milk powder. Stir well to combine. Begin to whip the cream on medium high speed. As the cream thickens, gradually add the sugar and vanilla extract. Continue to beat the cream until stiff peaks form. Remove the bowl from the stand mixer and fold in the mango pieces.

ASSEMBLY

With a 3-inch round cookie cutter, begin to cut out circles from the sheet cake. You should be able to make eight 3-layer cakelets. Spoon the mango cream onto each layer of the cakelets. Garnish the top layer with cream and upright slices of mango.

These cakes can be kept in the refrigerator for up to 3 days or can be frozen for up to 1 month, without garnish. To freeze: place the individual cakes on a baking sheet in the freezer. When frozen, wrap in plastic wrap, then in aluminum foil.

Light as Air Angel Food Cake

Preparation Time: 20 minutes / **Baking Time:** 35 to 40 minutes

Equipment: *One 10-inch tube pan, ungreased, a stand mixer fitted with the whisk attachment or a handheld mixer.*

So many people just love angel food cake and it is probably one of my most popular birthday requests. Light as air, this cake just begs for the addition of fruit and whipped cream. If it were not for the fact that the batter takes 12 egg whites, I would be making this cake once a week. As it is, I now reserve this recipe for the birthdays of special friends. I have stabilized the whipped cream in this cake with gelatin for a longer lasting freshness. This is a good tip to have as you can bake cream filled desserts well in advance of when you need them. However, if you are serving on the same day, you can use regular whipped cream.

12 egg whites (I do not recommend using the carton of egg whites for this cake)

1½ cups sugar, divided

1 teaspoon cream of tartar

¼ teaspoon salt

2 teaspoons vanilla extract

1 cup cake flour, spooned and leveled

1 tablespoon of grated lemon rind

STABILIZED WHIPPED CREAM WITH FRESH BERRIES

2 cups whipping cream

½ cup icing sugar

1 teaspoon vanilla

1 packet or 2½ teaspoons gelatin

3 tablespoons of water

2 cups of fresh berries of your choice (strawberries, raspberries, blueberries)

Preheat the oven to 350°F. Combine ½ cup of sugar with the flour and sift these ingredients onto a piece of parchment paper.

Place the egg whites in a heatproof bowl over a saucepan of boiling water. There should be no more than 2 inches of water in the saucepan. Warm the whites, stirring all the while, until they feel warm to the touch. Immediately pour the egg whites into the bowl of the stand mixer and start beating on medium high speed. When the egg whites are foamy add the salt and cream of tartar. Continue beating and as the egg whites begin to thicken, gradually add in the rest of the sugar. When the egg whites

Recipe continues on page 157

are at the soft peak stage, add in the vanilla and lemon zest. Continue beating until stiff peaks form. Remove the bowl from the stand. Tip in the flour and sugar mixture in 3 additions, folding well with a rubber spatula after each addition.

Pour the batter into the tube pan, using an offset spatula to smooth the top to the edges. Bake for 35 to 45 minutes or until a toothpick comes out clean. Turn the cake upside down on a rack and allow the cake to cool for 30 minutes. After 30 minutes, use a thin knife to loosen the sides of the pan and unfold the cake. Let cool completely before decorating.

STABILIZED WHIPPED CREAM WITH BERRIES

Place 3 tablespoons of cool water in a medium sized microwavable bowl and sprinkle one packet of gelatin over the water. Stir to combine and allow the gelatin to bloom for 5 minutes. After 5 minutes, microwave the gelatin for 10 seconds, then 5 seconds, until the gelatin dissolves. Gelatin cannot be boiled so be careful not to overheat. The gelatin should feel smooth, not grainy to the touch. Pour the whipping cream into the bowl of the stand mixer. Beat on medium high speed, gradually adding the icing sugar and vanilla as the cream thickens.

When the cream just begins to form stiff peaks, it is time to add the gelatin. Take out ½ cup of whipped cream and add it to the melted gelatin. Mix well. Then add the whipped cream and gelatin mixture back into the rest of the whipped cream. Continue beating until stiff peaks form. Remove the bowl from the stand and fold in one cup of the berries. You may want to cut the larger berries in half. Reserve some whole berries for the top of the cake.

ASSEMBLY

Cut the cake in half and spoon the whipped cream with berries onto one of the layers. Top with the remaining half and liberally spoon the rest of the cream with berries on top of the cake. Garnish with whole berries.

This cake will keep for up to three days in the refrigerator and can be frozen without the garnish for up to 1 month. To freeze: place the cake unwrapped on a baking sheet in the freezer. When frozen, wrap in plastic wrap, then in aluminum foil.

15 Layer Crepe Cake with Hazelnut (Nutella) Chocolate Ganache

Preparation Time: 1 hour / **Chilling Time:** 4 hours or overnight

Equipment: A non-stick skillet, preferably 8 inches in diameter, blender or stand mixer fitted with the whisk attachment, a large baking tray for holding the crepes, several pieces of waxed paper or aluminum foil to place between the cooked crepes.

For this recipe, you will need a good nonstick small frying pan. I chose an 8-inch pan. The crepes are only cooked for 30 seconds or so a side, but you do need a lot of them. I found the trick to turning the crepes over easily was to lift one corner of the crepe with a small offset spatula, which allowed a larger spatula to get under it and flip it over. This is a lovely light different tasting kind of cake. It goes well with a robust filling, which you can spread thinly over each layer. You do have to be careful to choose a filling of the right consistency, because if the filling is too liquid, the layers will tend to slide off of the cake. I know this because I first tried it with whipped cream and ended up with a cake in a puddle.

CREPES (Makes 16 to 18)
1½ cups milk
¼ cup butter (1 tablespoon more for brushing on the bottom of the frying pan)
6 large eggs, at room temperature
1 cup flour
¼ cup sugar
1 teaspoon vanilla
¼ teaspoon salt

HAZELNUT CHOCOLATE GANACHE
1 cup dark 54% Callebaut chocolate callets, Chipits or chopped chocolate (you will need two 70% 100-gram bars)
⅔ cup whipping cream
1 tablespoon butter
1½ cups Nutella
2 tablespoons unsweetened cocoa powder

HAZELNUT PRALINE GARNISH
(Optional)
½ cup raw hazelnuts
1 cup sugar
¼ cup water
1 tablespoon butter

CREPES

Sift the flour and salt onto a piece of parchment paper.

Place the butter and milk in a glass measuring cup or pitcher and warm in the microwave for 50 to 60 seconds, until the butter is melted. Pour into the bowl of the stand mixer. With the mixer on low, gradually add the sugar. Add the eggs one at a time, beating well, after each addition. Add the vanilla and salt. With the mixer on low, tip in the flour in three additions. Blend until well combined, scraping down to the bottom of the bowl with a spatula to ensure that all the ingredients have been fully incorporated. Pour into a large measuring cup or pitcher and place in the refrigerator for 30 minutes, before using.

Brush a small amount of butter over the bottom of a non-stick frying pan and heat on medium high. Pour slightly less than ¼ cup of batter into the skillet at one time, tilting the pan to evenly cover. When the crepe begins to bubble (about 30 seconds) lift the edge of the crepe with an offset spatula, place a larger spatula underneath and flip the crepe over to cook for another 30 seconds. The crepes should be lightly browned. Transfer the cooked crepes onto a parchment lined baking sheet. Note: I stack the crepes in small towers, with pieces of waxed paper in between the crepes. Once finished, you should have between 15 to 18 crepes, depending on the size of your pan. Refrigerate the crepes until cold.

HAZELNUT GANACHE FILLING

Place the chocolate and butter in a heat proof bowl. Simmer the cream in a saucepan and pour the hot cream over the chocolate. Wait 30 seconds and then stir until smooth. Add the Nutella, ½ cup at a time, stirring until incorporated. Sift 2 tablespoons of cocoa powder over the chocolate filling, stirring until well blended. Let the ganache cool at room temperature, stirring every once and awhile, until it reaches a nice spreadable consistency.

HAZELNUT PRALINE GARNISH (OPTIONAL)

Have ready a parchment lined baking sheet. Place the sugar in a saucepan, adding the water, carefully. Bring the sugar syrup to a boil. Continue to boil until the caramel reaches a rich amber color. Remove from the heat and stir in the butter. Add the hazelnuts and pour the mixture onto the baking sheet, spreading with an offset spatula. Once cool, break the brittle into jagged shaped pieces.

ASSEMBLY

Begin to stack the crepes. Place the first crepe on the plate which you will be using to serve as this is a difficult cake to move. Cover the crepe evenly in a thin layer of ganache, being careful to go just to the edges. Top with the next crepe and cover with ganache. Repeat this process until all the layers have been stacked and covered. Cover the topmost crepe with ganache but do not cover the sides of the cake. Garnish with hazelnut praline, orange zest or shaved chocolate. Refrigerate for at least 4 hours, before slicing.

This cake, without garnish, can be kept in the refrigerator for 4 days or can be frozen for up to 1 month. If freezing, place the cake unwrapped on a baking sheet in the freezer. When frozen, wrap in plastic wrap, then cover with aluminum foil. Thaw in the refrigerator on the day you will be serving.

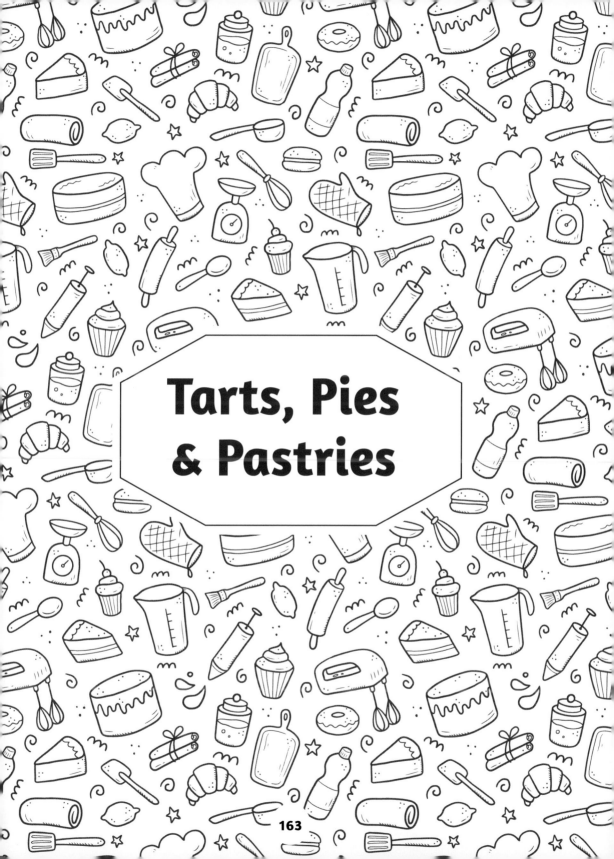

Tarts, Pies
& Pastries

A Lemon Cream Tart Worth Sharing

Preparation Time: 20 minutes / **Baking Time:** 18 to 20 minutes / **Chilling Time:** 1 hour

Equipment: *One 10-inch removable base tart pan; food processor, pie weights (commercial weights or dried beans) for blind baking the crust.*

This lemon tart is made with a lemon curd that is cooked over the stove top for a short period of time, then poured into a partially blind-baked shell and baked for a brief period of time. Cream is incorporated into the lemon curd a minute or so before it is taken off the stove, which allows the cream to mix with the filling, without separating. The result is a lemon tart with a perfect citrus tang and creamy texture. Topped with fresh berries, it is a wonderful finish to any dinner.

SHORTCRUST PASTRY
(Partially Blind-Baked)

2½ cups flour

2 tablespoons sugar

½ teaspoon salt

1 cup cold butter cut into cubes

1 teaspoon vanilla extract

1 teaspoon of lemon juice

¼ cup ice cold water

1 whisked egg white for coating
    the baked shell

LEMON FILLING

8 large egg yolks, room temperature

1¼ cups sugar

⅔ cup lemon juice
    (juice from 4 large lemons)

Zest from 1 lemon
    (zest before squeezing)

½ cup butter cubed

¼ cup whipping cream
    (warmed in the microwave,
    but not hot)

GARNISH
Fresh berries marinated in Chambord
    liqueur (optional, see page 246)

SHORTCRUST PASTRY

Place the flour, sugar, and salt in the bowl of a food processor. Pulse to combine.

Add the cold cubed butter and pulse, in short intervals, until the butter is dispersed throughout the dough in large pea size pieces. Add the vanilla extract and lemon juice to ¼ cup very cold water. Take the lid off the processor and dribble the water over the flour. Pulse just until the dough begins to come together. Dump the ragged dough out onto a floured piece of parchment paper or into a large mixing bowl. With floured hands, knead the dough until it comes together into a smooth ball. You can add up to 1 more tablespoon of water, if needed. Form two thirds of the dough into a disk and refrigerate for 60 minutes. The remaining dough can be made into a smaller disk and put into the fridge or freezer for a later use, such as pastry cookies (see recipe under Thanksgiving Pumpkin Tarts on page 185).

Bring out the pastry dough 15 minutes before you plan to roll it. Roll out the dough between two sheets of waxed paper to between ⅛ and ¼ inch thickness and to a size an inch larger than that of your tart pan. Lift the dough up periodically and re-flour the surface underneath to make sure the dough is not sticking to the paper. Lift the dough over the rolling pin and use the rolling pin to position the circle of dough over the tart pan. Gently coax the dough into the bottom and up the sides of the pan. Remove any overhang by pressing down on the edges of the tart pan with the rolling pin. Chill the lined tart pan in the freezer for 15 minutes.

PARTIALLY BLIND-BAKING THE TART SHELL

Preheat the oven to 400°F. Place the tart shell on a cookie sheet. Line the tart shell with a piece of slightly crumpled up parchment paper. Add commercial pie weights or dried beans to the lined tart shell making sure they go right up to the rim. Bake on a cookie sheet in the preheated oven for 15 minutes. Bring the shell out of the oven and carefully remove the weights and parchment paper. Prick the shell all over with the tines of a fork. Place the shell back in the oven for another 5 minutes until the bottom of the pastry is lightly browned. Remove the pie shell from the oven and, while still warm, brush the bottom of the crust with a whisked egg white. This will prevent the crust from going soggy when filled. Let the shell cool for 15 minutes before filling.

Recipe continues on page 167

LEMON FILLING

Turn down the oven heat to 330°F. In a medium sized saucepan off the heat, whisk together the egg yolks. Gradually add the sugar and zest and keep whisking just until the sugar is incorporated. Warm the lemon juice in the microwave for 30 seconds (it should be warm but not hot) and slowly whisk the lemon juice into the egg mixture.

Place the saucepan on the burner and heat over medium low heat, whisking constantly, just until the lemon curd begins to thicken (about 5 to 7 minutes). Do not let it boil. Add the butter and continue to stir. Warm the whipping cream in the microwave for 25 seconds and stream the warmed whipping cream into the lemon curd, whisking the curd for approximately 1 more minute, until the cream is well incorporated.

Pour the mixture through a sieve into a large measuring cup and then pour the curd into your pie shell. Place the tart in the oven and bake for approximately 15 to 18 minutes or until the curd is set. Let cool on a wire rack, then place in the refrigerator for at least 2 hours, before serving. Garnish with fresh fruit, if using.

This tart can be refrigerated for 3 days or frozen for up to 1 month. It is best, if freezing, to decorate with fruit the day of serving. To freeze: Place the cooled tart on a baking sheet in the freezer. When frozen, wrap in plastic wrap, then in aluminum foil.

Date Night Chocolate Praline Tart

Preparation Time: 60 minutes / **Baking Time:** 20 to 25 minutes

Equipment: *One 10-inch removable base tart pan, or pie plate, a stand mixer fitted with the paddle attachment or a handheld mixer.*

This recipe is made with a chocolate ganache and is unique in that it infuses orange peel in the heated whipping cream to give the chocolate filling a subtle hint of citrus. The chopped maple pecans on top of the chocolate crust add a lovely crunch. If you want to go all out, garnish the tart with candied orange slices (see recipe under Citrus Slices in Syrup on page 249). This reinforces the subtle orange flavor in the filling and looks stunning against the dark chocolate. However, the tart is lovely served just with some cocoa sifted on top.

CHOCOLATE CRUMB CRUST

1½ cups Oreo chocolate baking crumbs

½ cup almond or hazelnut flour

½ cup butter, melted

½ cup dark 54% chocolate Callebaut callets or Chipits

2 tablespoons white sugar

Pinch of salt

Maple pecans (see recipe under Banana Cake, page 100)

FILLING

¾ cup cream

½ cup butter cubed

Shaved peel of 1 orange (avoid pith)

12 ounces or 2 cups of dark 54% Callebaut callets or Chipits or 70% chocolate finely chopped (four 100-gram bars)

2 large eggs, plus 4 large egg yolks, at room temperature

½ cup granulated sugar

Pinch of salt

GARNISH

3 tablespoons sifted cocoa powder

Whipped cream or crème fraiche for serving (see Cheat Crème Fraiche, page 253)

Orange slices in syrup (optional, see Citrus Slices in Syrup on page 249)

CHOCOLATE CRUMB CRUST

Preheat the oven to 350°F. Combine the chocolate crumbs with the nut flour, chocolate, and sugar. Note: Adding nut flours and chocolate to crumb pastry crusts helps to prevent them from going soggy over time. Add the melted butter and mix well. The chocolate chips will melt a little and this is fine. Press into the tart pan and bake for 8 to 10 minutes until set. Let cool in the refrigerator. When ready to fill, sprinkle evenly with chopped maple pecans.

FILLING

Preheat the oven to 350°F. Place the cream, butter, and orange peel in a small saucepan over low heat until the butter has melted. Let the cream simmer for 2 minutes. Remove from the heat and allow the orange peel to steep in the warm milk for 20 minutes. Place the chocolate in a heat proof bowl. Reheat the cream/butter mixture until it comes to a simmer. Then, using a sieve, strain the hot cream over the chocolate. Wait 30 seconds and then stir the chocolate until the chocolate mixture is silky and smooth. Set aside to cool.

Place the eggs and yolks in the bowl of a stand mixer. Beat on medium speed. As the eggs begin to thicken, gradually add the sugar. Continue beating on high speed, until the eggs have become pale and increased in volume. Remove the bowl from the stand and gently fold the cooled chocolate mixture into the egg mixture, one third at a time.

Chop up the pecans and sprinkle over the crust. Scrape the chocolate filling into the tart shell over the pecan pieces. Bake the tart for 20 to 25 minutes. The chocolate should be set; however, it is fine to have a slight wobble in the center. Remove it from the oven and let cool. Sift cocoa powder over the tart. Garnish with orange slices, if using.

This tart keeps well in the refrigerator for up to 3 days and can be frozen, without garnish, for up to 2 months. If freezing, place the tart unwrapped on a baking sheet in the freezer. When frozen, wrap in plastic wrap, then in aluminum foil.

Mile High Apple Filo Pie

Preparation Time: 45 minutes / **Baking Time:** 1 hour

Equipment: *One 8- or 9-inch springform pan, pastry brush.*

This is a great pie to make in the height of apple season as it takes a lot of apples. It is easy to prepare, but because you are making this in a 9-inch springform pan, it does require more apples than a traditional pie. I used ten large Honeycrisp apples and the springform pan was only ¾ of the way full. The apples are sliced thinly and layered in circles all the way to the top. They maintain their crispness, even after being cooked, and sit perfectly inside the crispy filo crust. This is a delightful dessert to share for any occasion and transports easily from one home to another.

FILLING

8 to 10 Honeycrisp apples or any good baking apple

¾ cup sugar

⅓ cup butter at room temperature, broken up into small pieces

1 tablespoon lemon juice

1 teaspoon cinnamon

¼ teaspoon nutmeg

2 tablespoons of flour

PASTRY

1 box of filo pastry, thawed, but cold

½ cup butter melted with 2 teaspoons of water

½ cup sugar for sprinkling over the filo

2 tablespoons of almond flour

APPLE ROSE GARNISH
(Optional)

1 apple thinly sliced

2 tablespoons of icing sugar for dusting on the top of the pie

APPLES

Peel and slice the apples thinly, approximately ¼ of an inch thick. Place the slices in a large mixing bowl. Add the sugar, lemon juice, 2 tablespoons of flour, cinnamon, and nutmeg. Make sure the flour is well incorporated into the apples. The butter will be added later as you layer the apples in the filo pastry.

FILO ASSEMBLY

Note: You have to work quickly as filo pastry can dry out in minutes. If you want to take your time, place a damp dish towel over the filo you are not using, as you are working. Because filo is fragile, I always keep a spare box in my fridge in case some of the filo gets torn or becomes too dry to work with near the end.

Melt the butter with the water in the microwave. Brush the bottom and sides of the springform pan generously with the melted butter. Working with two sheets of filo at a time, unfold the sheets and brush melted butter along the entire surface of the top sheet. Sprinkle the top sheet with sugar. With the long side facing you, fold the ends of the double filo layer into the center of the sheet. Fold one end over the other. You will now have 8 layers of filo in a strip.

Brush the top of the folded length of filo with butter and sprinkle with sugar. Sugar side up, place one end of the folded filo strip into the center of the springform pan, allowing the rest of the strip of filo to run along the bottom of the pan and drape over the edge of the outside rim. Make sure you tuck the filo strip into the rounded bottom edge of the pan.

Repeat this process with the next two sheets of filo and continue until you have covered the entire bottom and rim of your springform pan with filo strips. The strips will slightly overlap each other.

Preheat the oven to 350°F. Sprinkle 2 tablespoons of almond flour on the bottom of your pastry. This will soak up any excess juices from the apples and help keep the bottom of your filo pastry crisp. Begin placing the first layer of apples on the bottom of the pan, working your way from the outside into the center, overlapping the apple slices, slightly. After two layers of apples, dot with small pieces of butter. Continue until you have used up all your apple slices, dotting with butter every two layers. Then, begin to fold all your filo strips over the apples into the center, beginning with the first strip of filo that you placed. If you feel that you have too much filo at the top of your pan, simply trim the ends of the filo with scissors.

Brush the top of the filo pie with melted butter and sprinkle it with sugar. For decoration, you can scrunch up a smaller piece of filo and place it on the top, brush it with melted butter and sprinkle it with sugar. It looks somewhat like a rose. If you want to get fancy, you can make an actual apple rose garnish (recipe follows).

Bake the pie for 50 minutes to 1 hour. If the top is getting too browned after 40 minutes, loosely cover the pan with aluminum foil. When cool, you can dust the pie with icing sugar.

This pie can be kept in the refrigerator for 3 days or can be frozen for up to 1 month. To freeze: place the cold pie on a baking sheet, unwrapped. When frozen, wrap in plastic wrap, then in aluminum foil.

APPLE ROSE GARNISH

Core and slice an apple into very thin slices (⅛ inch) with the skin on. Place the apple slices in a bowl of salt and cover well with the salt. This will soften the slices. When soft, rinse off the salt and place the apple slices slightly overlapping each other in a row, skin side on the bottom of the row. The row will look like a scalloped edge. Roll up the row from one end to the other which will make an apple rose shape. Place four toothpicks in the rose to hold its shape. You can add more slices onto the toothpicks as needed for a fuller rose shape.

Apple Galette

Preparation Time: 30 minutes / **Chilling Time:** 45 minutes / **Baking Time:** 40 minutes

Equipment: *A food processor fitted with a steel blade, a 12 x 18-inch cookie sheet lined with parchment paper.*

The simplest of all apple pies and just as good tasting is the apple galette. Your work is cut in half as it consists of only one crust, rolled out and shaped for filling with the fruit. Furthermore, it is *supposed* to be rustic looking. There is no need to roll out a perfect circle of dough or have neat and tidy edges. The galette is a wonderful dessert to bring to outdoor barbecues and picnics as it is easily cut into rectangles or wedges and eaten like a hand pie.

1 shortcrust pie pastry (see recipe under A Lemon Tart Worth Sharing, page 164)

Egg wash (1 egg whisked with 2 teaspoons of water)

2 tablespoons of turbinado sugar

FILLING

6 to 8 Honeycrisp apples, sliced into ¼ inch slices

2 tablespoons almond flour

BRUSH ON SAUCE FOR APPLES

2 tablespoons butter

4 tablespoons apple or peach juice

2 tablespoons sugar

2 tablespoons brandy (optional)

Preheat the oven to 365°F. Prepare the dough according to the recipe on page 164. You will need only ⅔ of the pastry dough for the galette so you can either freeze the unused pastry or make pastry cookies with the leftover dough (see recipe for pastry cookies under Thanksgiving Pumpkin Tarts, page 185). Chill the disk of dough for the galette for 45 minutes before rolling.

Roll out the chilled pastry to a 13-inch oval or circular shape, approximately ¼ inch in thickness. Sprinkle the almond flour evenly over the crust. Place the apples on top of the pastry, leaving a 1½ inch border. You can layer the apples anyway you like, overlapping in a circular pattern or overlapping in rows.

Make the sauce by combining all the ingredients in a small saucepan and allowing the sauce to simmer for 5 minutes. Brush the warm sauce generously over the apples. Fold the edges of the crust over the filling, making pleats in the pastry, where needed. Brush the crust with egg wash and sprinkle with turbinado sugar. Bake for 45 to 50 minutes or until the crust is nicely browned. Once baked, you can brush the cooked apples once more with the sauce, if desired. The galette will keep in the refrigerator for three days or can be frozen for one month.

Bourbon Butter Tarts

Preparation Time: 30 minutes / **Chilling Time:** 45 minutes / **Baking Time:** 20 to 25 minutes

Equipment: *A food processor fitted with the steel blade, a standard 12 cup muffin tin, pie weights or dried beans for blind baking the tart shells. 12 cupcake liners.*

There are three main camps for butter tarts, runny or firm, with raisins or without, with nuts or without. Well, these butter tarts have raisins with a qualifier. The raisins are soaked in bourbon. Even if you previously disliked raisins in your butter tarts, give these butter tarts a try. The bourbon adds another dimension of flavor to the raisins and changes their texture. The soaked raisins almost melt into the filling. These butter tarts are not firm, but they are not super runny, either. You can pick one up and eat it quickly and surreptitiously without the inside of the tart running down your face. No one will notice. Which is of course why I like them. I have avoided using nuts as these tarts often go to school (without the bourbon, of course,) and work fundraisers. This recipe makes 12 tarts. Note: You can use any liquor of choice in the filling. I often use rum or brandy, and, of course, you can omit it, altogether.

SHORTCRUST PASTRY

2½ cups flour

1 cup cold cubed butter

½ teaspoon salt

1 tablespoon sugar

1 teaspoon of lemon juice

¼ cup ice cold water

FILLING

1 cup brown sugar

½ cup corn syrup

3 large eggs, at room temperature

1 teaspoon vanilla

1 teaspoon lemon juice

¼ teaspoon salt

¾ cup melted salted butter

¼ cup whipping cream

1 cup raisins

4 tablespoons bourbon

RAISINS

Place the bourbon and the raisins in a small saucepan. Cook on medium heat until the mixture comes to a simmer. Let the mixture simmer for 1 minute, then remove from the heat and set aside to allow the raisins to absorb the alcohol.

PASTRY

Place the flour, sugar, and salt in the food processor. Pulse to combine. Scatter the cold cubes of butter over the flour. Pulse in short intervals, until the butter has been distributed throughout the dough in large pea size pieces. Combine the lemon juice and cold water. Take the lid off of the food processor and dribble the liquid around the flour. Pulse again two or three times, in brief intervals. The dough should be coming together, but still look ragged. Scrape the mixture out onto a large piece of floured parchment paper or into a large mixing bowl. With floured hands knead the dough until it comes together. If the dough is very dry, you can add up to one more tablespoon of water to it. Shape the dough into two 8-inch logs. Wrap the logs and refrigerate for 45 minutes.

With a sharp knife, slice each log of dough into 6 pieces. On a floured surface, roll each piece of dough into a 4 to 5-inch circle of between ⅛ and ¼ inch thickness. You can use a 4 or 5-inch round cookie cutter to cut out more precise circles. Line each muffin cup with the pastry. You will have some ruffles or creases in the pastry at the top which I think looks quite pretty. Continue rolling out the dough until you have filled the muffin tin. Place the pastry lined muffin tray in the freezer for 15 minutes.

PARTIALLY BLIND BAKING THE PASTRY

Preheat the oven to 400°F. Note: This is a step that you can miss and go straight to filling the tart shells. However, I admittedly have an obsession about soggy pastry and I find with butter tarts the filling often is cooked before the bottom of the tarts are fully browned. Consequently, I blind-bake the tart shells. If you want to disregard this step, I understand (I guess).

Using large cupcake liners (I use parchment paper liners) line the pastry cups and fill each cup with dried commercial weights or beans. Bake the pastry for 15 minutes. Carefully, remove the liners and weights, prick the pastry all over with the tines of a fork, and bake the pastry cups for 5 more minutes. Set aside.

FILLING

With a hand whisk, combine the brown sugar, corn syrup and melted butter together in a mixing bowl. In a smaller bowl, whisk the eggs and then add the eggs to the butter/sugar mixture. Add the lemon juice and vanilla. Whisk in the cream until it is fully incorporated. Add ¼ teaspoon salt. Pour the filling from the mixing bowl into a spouted jug or large measuring cup. Place 1 heaping teaspoon of marinated raisins at the bottom of each muffin cup. Fill each tart shell almost to the top with the filling.

Reduce the oven temperature to 375°F. Bake for 20 to 23 minutes. You will see the butter tarts begin to dome at around 18 minutes. At this point you can remove the tarts for a runny filling or bake for a few minutes longer, for a firmer consistency.

Butter tarts will keep in airtight containers in the refrigerator for 5 days or in the freezer for 2 months. To freeze: freeze cooled tarts unwrapped on a baking sheet. When frozen, cover with wax paper and place in airtight containers.

Cherry Frangipane Tarts with Blackcurrant Jam

Preparation Time: 30 minutes / **Baking Time:** 30 minutes

Equipment: *Eight individual removable rim tart pans, or one 10-inch removable rim tart pan, buttered and floured, a food processor fitted with a steel blade.*

It was only later in life that I came to appreciate frangipane or sweet almond cream and when I did discover its amazing taste and texture, I began to put it in everything bakeable. This tart is equally good made with sliced pears or peaches, but I just love the look and taste of fresh cherries in season. The base of the tart is made with shortcrust pastry, then filled with the frangipane. I chose to make this recipe using small, individual removable tart pans; however, you can just as easily make one large tart in a 10-inch removable tart pan.

1 Shortcrust Pastry, Partially Blind-Baked (see recipe under Bourbon Butter Tarts, page 176)

ALMOND CREAM

½ cup salted butter at room temperature

½ cup sugar

1 teaspoon vanilla extract

½ teaspoon almond extract

2 large eggs at room temperature

1 cup almond flour

¼ teaspoon salt

½ cup of good quality black currant jam for spreading on the bottom of the tart.

CHERRIES

1½ pounds fresh Bing cherries, washed and pitted (I use a small hand size cherry pitter for this job)

PASTRY

Line the tart shells with parchment paper and blind-bake the pastry, according to instructions for Bourbon Butter Tarts on page 176. You may need to roll out larger circles for your individual tart pans. If using only one tart pan, roll out the pastry to a 12-inch circle. Let the pastry cool before filling.

CHERRIES

Reserve 16 whole cherries, 8 with their stems on, and cut the rest of the cherries in half. Lightly flour the cut cherries.

ALMOND CREAM FILLING

Preheat the oven to 350°F. In the bowl of the food processor, pulse together the butter, sugar, and eggs until creamy. Add the extracts and the salt. Tip in the almond flour and pulse until the almond cream is smooth. Spread jam over the bottom of each cooled partially baked tart shell.

Then, fill the tarts with the almond cream. Place about eight cherries decoratively around the top of the tart, cut side down. Place one whole cherry in the center of the tart. After baking, you can replace this cooked cherry with a fresh stemmed cherry for a pretty presentation. Bake for about 30 minutes or until the frangipane is golden brown. When out of the oven brush the top of the tart with warm apricot jam mixed with a 1 teaspoon of lemon juice (optional).

These tarts can be refrigerated in airtight containers for up to 3 days or frozen for up to 1 month. If freezing, brush the tops of the tarts with the apricot glaze but do not place a fresh cherry on top until you are ready to serve.

Portuguese Custard Tarts

Preparation Time: 30 minutes / **Chilling Time:** 1 hour / **Baking Time:** 12 minutes

---

Equipment: *Rolling pin, a medium-large saucepan, digital read food thermometer, 12 cup muffin tin, greased, and lightly floured.*

I love Portuguese custard tarts and this recipe is made easier by using store-bought puff pastry. The traditional pastry for this tart, which is similar to making a rough puff pastry, is very time consuming. However, I honestly can say that the quality of this tart still is excellent with a flakiness to the crust and a texture, taste and creaminess to the filling that is the signature of a real Portuguese tart. This recipe is made by pouring a hot syrup into a custard and you will need a digital read thermometer to obtain the exact temperature of the syrup.

CRUST

1 "All Butter" package of frozen puff
  pastry, thawed but cold

2 tablespoons melted butter

CUSTARD BASE

1 cup milk

1 cup cream

⅓ cup flour

6 large egg yolks at room temperature

¼ teaspoon of nutmeg

¼ teaspoon salt

2 teaspoons vanilla extract

SUGAR SYRUP

¾ cup sugar

¼ cup water

1 cinnamon stick

Slices of lemon peel from
  1 large lemon

CRUST

On a lightly floured piece of parchment or wax paper roll out a sheet of puff pastry into a 13-inch square. The dough should be as thin as you can get it without tearing it. With a pastry brush, brush melted butter over the entire square. Roll up the sheet of pastry into a tight cylinder and cover with plastic wrap. Chill for 1 hour. Unwrap the dough, trim the ends and cut into 12 pieces. Roll out each piece of dough into a circle and fit the pastry rounds into the molds of the prepared muffin tin. Trim off the excess dough around each muffin cup with a pair of scissors. Place the muffin tin in the freezer while you prepare the custard. **Preheat the oven to 500°F.**

Recipe continues on page 184

CUSTARD

Place the egg yolks into a medium sized bowl. Whisk together the flour and salt in a large heavy bottomed saucepan. Add ⅓ cup of cold milk to the flour and continue whisking until a smooth paste has formed. Gradually add the rest of the milk and cream, still whisking, until all of the milk/cream has been incorporated. Add the nutmeg and cook over medium heat, stirring constantly, until the milk has thickened and just come to a boil. Remove from the heat. Gradually, whisk ½ cup of the hot milk into the egg yolks and add the egg yolks back into the remaining milk/cream, whisking constantly. Remember that now the saucepan is off the heat. Add the vanilla and strain the custard into a large measuring cup or pitcher. Set aside.

SYRUP

Place the sugar in a small saucepan and pour the water evenly over the sugar being careful not to splash the sides of the pan. Add the cinnamon stick and lemon peel. Bring the syrup to a boil, stirring occasionally. When the syrup reaches 212°F or 100°C, remove from the heat. Let cool for 10 minutes. Then, strain the syrup into the still warm custard, mixing well to incorporate.

Pour the custard into the muffin cups, filling ¾ full. Bake for approximately 12 minutes or until the custard has started to blister and caramelize and the pastry has browned considerably. If this is not achieved in bake mode, you can finish the tarts under the broiler, but be careful not to burn the pastry. You also can use a small blow torch to finish caramelizing the tops of the tarts. The tops of the tarts can be sprinkled with sugar before you torch them.

These tarts can be kept in airtight containers in the fridge for 4 days or can be frozen for up to 1 month. To freeze: place cooled tarts unwrapped on a baking sheet. When frozen, wrap in wax paper before placing in an airtight container.

Pumpkin Tarts with Sour Cream Glaze

Preparation Time: 30 minutes / **Chilling Time:** 45 minutes / **Baking Time:** 35 minutes

Equipment: *A 12-cup muffin tin, lightly sprayed with Pam or greased with butter, a food processor fitted with the steel blade, a rolling pin.*

This is a perfect Thanksgiving recipe and it can make several tarts or 1 large deep-dish pie. I have added a touch of pepper to the pumpkin filling, which you cannot readily detect, but still lends a pleasing spicy note to the filling. I also have incorporated orange zest which combines well with the warmth of the ginger and lends a citrus note to the tart. The pastry is the same shortcrust used in the recipe for Bourbon Butter Tarts, however, feel free to use store bought.

1 Shortcrust Pastry (see recipe under
  Bourbon Butter Tarts, page 176)

FILLING

3 large eggs at room temperature, lightly
  beaten
1 (15-ounce) can of pure pumpkin puree
  (unsweetened) or 2 cups
1¼ cups evaporated milk
1 cup dark brown sugar
2 teaspoons of ginger
¼ teaspoon of black pepper
½ teaspoon salt
¼ teaspoon of allspice
½ teaspoon of cinnamon
Zest of 1 large orange
2 tablespoons of flour

SOUR CREAM GLAZE

1 cup sour cream
¼ cup white sugar

PASTRY COOKIES FOR GARNISH
  (Optional)

Cold leftover pastry
Egg wash (1 large egg whisked with
  2 teaspoon of water)
Sugar, white or turbinado, to be sprinkled
  over the cookies

PASTRY

Follow the instructions for shortcrust pastry under Bourbon Butter Tarts (page 176). Partially blind-bake in the same way.

FILLING

Preheat the oven to 350°F. In a large bowl, whisk together the eggs, pumpkin puree, sugar, and evaporated milk, until smooth. Add the spices, salt, and orange zest. Remove about ¼ cup of the filling and whisk it in with the flour. Whisk the flour mixture back into the rest of the filling making sure to get rid of any lumps. Pour the filling into a large measuring cup. Fill each muffin cup almost to the top, leaving less than a ¼ inch margin. The pumpkin filling will dome but will not flow over the top of the tart. Bake for approximately 30 minutes. Set aside.

SOUR CREAM GLAZE

Raise the oven temperature to 400°F. Mix together the sour cream with the sugar. Allow the tarts to cool for 20 minutes, before topping with the sour cream. Spoon the sour cream onto the top of each tart and smooth with an offset spatula. Place the tarts back in the oven for 5 to 7 minutes until the sour cream has set, but still is white. The sour cream will lose its shine and will not run when you lift the tin.

Unmold the tarts from the tin after 20 minutes and let cool at room temperature or in the refrigerator. You can garnish the tarts with small pastry cookies (see recipe below) and/or whipped cream.

PASTRY COOKIES

Cut out small shapes from the cold leftover pastry, brush with egg wash, sprinkle with sugar and bake at 375°F for 10 minutes or until lightly browned.

These tarts will keep in airtight containers in the refrigerator for 3 days or in the freezer for 2 months. To freeze: Place individual cooled tarts on a baking sheet, unwrapped. When frozen, wrap in waxed paper before placing in the container.

Mango Chocolate Tarts

Preparation Time: 1 hour / **Chilling Time** (Curd)**:** 4 hours

Equipment: *Six to eight individual removable rim tart pans, a food processor fitted with a steel blade, a stand mixer fitted with the paddle attachment or handheld mixer, a rolling pin.*

This tart is made with a chocolate shortbread crust, which bookends a dark chocolate ganache topping. Sandwiched in between is a beautiful tart mango curd and the combination is outstanding. The tarts have a long shelf life and boxed individually or in pairs make wonderful special occasions gifts.

CHOCOLATE SHORTBREAD CRUST

1 cup butter at room temperature

½ cup sugar

½ cup unsweetened cocoa powder

2 cups flour, scooped and leveled

½ teaspoon salt

MANGO CURD

2 cups chopped ripe mango (any variety of ripe mango is fine, I used Ataúlfo)

¼ cup lime juice

⅓ cup sugar plus 2 tablespoons, divided

½ cup butter

4 yolks and 2 whole eggs at room temperature

CHOCOLATE GANACHE TOPPING

1½ cups Callebaut 54% dark callets, Chipits or chopped chocolate (you will need three 100-gram 70% bars)

¾ cup whipping cream

2 tablespoons butter

1 tablespoon corn syrup

CRUST

In the bowl of a stand mixer fitted with the paddle attachment, cream together the butter and sugar until light and fluffy. On a large piece of parchment paper, whisk together the flour and salt. Sift in the cocoa powder. Tip the dry ingredients into the butter mixture and mix until fully incorporated. Scrape the dough out onto a floured piece of parchment or wax paper and bring the dough together into 2 disks.

Recipe continues on the next page

Refrigerate for 30 minutes. Roll out the dough between lightly floured sheets of waxed paper. With a round 4 to 5-inch cookie cutter (depending on the size of your individual tart pans) cut out circles ¼ inch thick and line the tart pans, making sure the pastry comes right up the sides to the top of the rim. Trim with your rolling pin. Place the lined tarts on a baking sheet and place in the freezer for 15 minutes. Any extra pastry can be frozen for later use.

Preheat the oven to 330°F. Bake the tarts for 20 to 25 minutes, until the pastry loses its shine. Let cool at room temperature for 15 minutes, then refrigerate until cold.

MANGO CURD

Place the chopped mango, lime juice and ⅓ cup sugar in the bowl of a food processor. Pulse until smooth. In a medium saucepan, melt the butter and set aside. Whisk the eggs with 2 tablespoons of sugar and add to the warm butter, whisking well. Add the pureed mango. Return to the heat and continue to whisk the mango curd over medium low heat until the mixture thickens. Do not boil. This will take from 7 to 10 minutes. When the mango curd is thick enough that a finger leaves a trail on the back of a spoon, remove from the heat, and let cool at room temperature for 15 minutes, stirring occasionally. Place plastic wrap directly on the curd and refrigerate, until cold and thick.

CHOCOLATE GANACHE

Place the chocolate, butter, and corn syrup in a heat proof bowl. In a saucepan, bring the cream to a simmer. Pour the hot cream over the chocolate. Wait for 30 seconds, then stir the chocolate until smooth and shiny. Set aside to cool, stirring occasionally.

ASSEMBLY

Fill the tart shells with the cold curd. With an offset spatula, spread the ganache over the top of the tarts. Allow the ganache to set at room temperature for 2 hours or in the refrigerator for 1 hour. Garnish with whipped cream and mango slices. These tarts keep well in airtight containers in the refrigerator for 5 days or can be frozen for up to one month. If freezing, place the tarts on a baking sheet, unwrapped. When frozen, wrap individually in waxed paper before placing in containers.

Maple Syrup Pecan Pie

Preparation Time: 30 minutes / **Chilling Time:** 45 minutes / **Baking Time:** 50 minutes

Equipment: *One 9- or 10-inch pie plate, food processor fitted with the paddle attachment.*

Rich with toasted pecans, maple syrup and brown sugar, this pie is a family favorite. I coaxed this recipe out of my 90-year-old neighbor, who occasionally would bring her coveted pie over to my house as a special treat. As she dropped it off, she would always smile with delight and say, "Pecans were on sale this week."

SHORTCRUST PASTRY

½ cup butter, cold and cubed

½ cup Crisco vegetable shortening, cold and cubed

2½ cups flour

2 tablespoons sugar

½ teaspoon salt

¼ cup cold water and up to 1 tablespoon more, if needed

2 teaspoons lemon juice

1 whisked egg white to brush on the pie crust after baking

FILLING

4 eggs and 1 yolk at room temperature

1 cup brown sugar

¾ cup maple syrup

¼ cup corn syrup

2 tablespoons flour

1½ cups pecan halves, toasted

½ teaspoon salt

2 teaspoons vanilla

½ teaspoon pure maple extract

PIE CRUST (Partially Blind-Baked)

Place the flour, salt, and sugar in the bowl of the food processor and pulse to combine. Add in the cold cubed butter and shortening and pulse in very short 5 second intervals until the fat is dispersed in large pea sized pieces. Combine the vanilla, lemon juice and cold water. Take the lid of the food processor and dribble over the flour. Pulse just until the dough begins to come together. It will look ragged. Scrape the dough out onto a large piece of floured parchment paper or into a large bowl and knead by hand until you can make the dough into a smooth round ball. You will need ¾ of the dough to make the pie crust. The remaining dough can be reserved for pastry cookies (see recipe under Pumpkin Tarts with Sour Cream Glaze, page 185) or a decorative rope around the pie crust. Refrigerate the disks for 30 to 45 minutes.

Recipe continues on page 193

Between sheets of lightly floured waxed paper, roll out the larger disk of dough to a thickness between ⅛ and ¼ inch and a diameter 1½ inches larger than your pie plate. Using your rolling pin, lift the pastry and center it over your pie plate. Gently coax the crust up the sides of your dish. There should be a ½ inch overhang. Fold the extra crust under itself and crimp or flute the edges of the pie. Place the lined pie plate in the freezer for 15 minutes.

Preheat the oven to 400°F. Crumple up a piece of parchment paper and fully line the unbaked crust. Fill with commercial pie weights or dried beans. Bake for 15 minutes. Remove the parchment paper and prick the crust all over with the tines of a fork. Bake for another 7 minutes until the bottom crust is just beginning to brown. Brush the bottom of the crust with a whisked egg white.

FILLING

Reduce the oven temperature to 350°F. Spread the pecan halves out on a parchment lined baking sheet and toast for 7 minutes. Reserve ¼ cup of the pecans for the top of the pie. Scatter the rest of the pecans over the warm pie crust.

Raise the oven temperature to 365°F. Combine the maple syrup, corn syrup, brown sugar, vanilla, maple extract and salt in a large bowl. Whisk the eggs and yolk together and add to the maple syrup mixture. Remove ½ cup of the filling and combine well with the flour. Add the flour mixture back into the rest of the filling, whisking well. Pour the filling over the pecans. Some of the pecans will become displaced as they float to the top so use your remaining pecan halves to fill in any gaps. Place your pie on the middle rack of the oven. Bake for approximately 50 to 60 minutes until the filling is set, with a very slight wobble in the center. If the crust begins to brown too much after 25 minutes, tent the pie with aluminum foil and continue baking. I used a deep-dish pie plate and consequently my cooking time was longer, and the cooking time will depend on the depth of your dish. It is best to check after 45 minutes. Let cool at room temperature for 1 hour before refrigerating. Slice when cold.

GARNISH

Serve the pie warm with pastry cookies, ice cream or whipped cream.

This pie will keep in the refrigerator for up to 5 days and can be frozen for up to 1 month. To freeze: place the cooled pie on a baking sheet in the freezer unwrapped. When frozen, wrap in plastic wrap, then aluminum foil.

Tropical Key Lime Tart with Pistachio Graham Cracker Crust

Preparation Time: 20 minutes / **Baking Time:** 18 to 20 minutes

Equipment: *One 9-inch pie plate, a stand mixer fitted with the whisk attachment or handheld mixer.*

This recipe calls for Persian limes (such an exotic sounding name, but they are the common limes you find at the supermarket), rather than key limes which are much smaller and paler in color. If you happen to have a bottle of key lime juice, feel free to substitute that for the Persian limes. Trader Joe's has a good tasting bottle of key lime juice. I have added ½ cup of finely chopped roasted pistachios to the graham cracker crumbs to make the crust for this pie. The saltiness of the pistachios goes well with the tartness of the limes and adds a nice bit of crunch to the crust. I have brought this tart to many a summer get-together and it makes all of us feel a little bit like we are on a summer "staycation."

GRAHAM PISTACHIO CRUST

1½ cups graham cracker crumbs

½ cup finely chopped shelled roasted pistachios (you can do this in a food processor)

½ cup butter, melted

¼ cup white sugar

FILLING

2 (14-ounce/300 ml) cans of sweetened condensed milk

2 large egg yolks at room temperature

1 cup sour cream

1 cup fresh lime juice from approximately 12 limes

1 tablespoon of lime zest

GARNISH

1 cup cold whipping cream

⅓ cup icing sugar

2 thinly sliced limes

CRUST

Preheat oven to 350°F. In a mixing bowl, combine the graham crackers, sugar and finely chopped pistachios. Pour in the melted butter and blend well. Press the crumbs firmly into the bottom and sides of the tart pan or pie plate. Bake the crust for 8 to 10 minutes, until lightly browned. Set aside to cool.

FILLING

In a large mixing bowl, whisk the egg yolks. Add the condensed milk, sour cream, and lime zest, mixing to a smooth consistency. Carefully stir in the juice until well incorporated. Pour the filling into the pie shell. Bake for 18 to 20 minutes, until the filling is just set. Let the tart come to room temperature and then refrigerate for at least 4 hours or overnight.

GARNISH

Beat the whipping cream until it begins to thicken. Reduce the speed to low and gradually add the icing sugar. Beat on high until stiff peaks form.

Pipe or dollop the whipping cream around the outside of the pie. Cut the lime slices in half and put a half slice of lime on each small mound of whipping cream.

This tart keeps well in the refrigerator for up to 4 days. It can be frozen without the garnish for up to 1 month. Freeze on a baking sheet, unwrapped. When frozen, wrap in plastic wrap, then in aluminum foil.

Frozen Dulce de Leche Pie with Chocolate Crumb Crust

Preparation Time: 30 minutes / **Freeze Time:** Overnight

Equipment: *1 deep dish 9 or 10-inch pie plate, buttered, a stand mixer fitted with the whisk and paddle attachment, or a handheld mixer.*

There is no denying that this is a sinfully indulgent dessert. But I tell myself, that if you cut a smaller slice, it all equals out. This recipe calls for dulce de leche which is mixed into a cream cheese filling. The caramel ends up forming a delicious sauce at the base of the pie. A garnish of fresh bananas, whipped cream and almond praline takes this pie to an ultimate level of indulgence. This is a fairly easy dessert to make and because it is frozen, you can simply relax, thaw and wait for the guests to arrive. Allow the pie to thaw on the counter for 20 minutes or in the refrigerator for 45 minutes, before serving.

CHOCOLATE CRUMB CRUST

1½ cups Oreo chocolate crumbs

½ cup melted butter

2 tablespoons sugar

½ cup dark 54% Callebaut chocolate callets or Chipits

DULCE DE LECHE FILLING

2 bricks of cream cheese (250 grams each), room temperature

2 (300-milliliter) tins of dulce de leche

1¼ cups whipping cream

⅓ cup sugar

¼ teaspoon salt

GARNISH

Sliced bananas

Whipped Cream

Almond Praline in Chocolate, (optional, page 248)

CRUST

Preheat the oven to 350°F. Combine the chocolate crumbs, chocolate and sugar in a mixing bowl. Pour the melted butter over the crumb mixture and combine thoroughly. The chips will melt but this is fine as it helps to hold the crust together. Pat into your prepared pie dish. Bake for 8 minutes. Set aside to cool. For faster cooling, you can place the crust in the freezer until you are ready to fill.

FILLING

Pour the whipping cream in the bowl of the stand mixer fitted with the whisk attachment. Whisk on high speed, adding the sugar in two additions as the cream begins to thicken. Continue beating until the cream forms stiff peaks. Remove the cream to a clean bowl and refrigerate. Clean out the stand mixer bowl and switch to the paddle attachment. Add the cream cheese to the bowl and beat on medium speed. When the cream cheese is smooth, add one tin of dulce de leche and ¼ teaspoon salt. Continue beating until the caramel is fully incorporated. Stop the mixer occasionally and scrape down to the bottom of the bowl with a spatula to make sure the cream cheese and caramel are being well incorporated. On low speed, fold in the cold whipped cream in two additions. When the whipped cream has been fully incorporated, pour the mixture into the prepared pie crust.

Open the second can of dulce de leche and evenly place small dollops (1 tablespoon each) over the top of the filling. With a toothpick or a knife blade, swirl through the dollops of caramel almost to the bottom of the pie crust, but not quite. This will make a pretty pattern, but it also will ensure that the caramel forms a sauce at the bottom of the pie. Freeze the pie overnight before serving. Place the pie unwrapped on a baking sheet. When frozen, wrap in plastic wrap, then in aluminum foil. This pie can keep well in the freezer for up to 1 month.

GARNISH

Garnish the pie with finely sliced bananas and whipped cream (whip 1 cup cream with ¼ cup sugar until stiff peaks form). You also can insert jagged pieces of chocolate almond praline around the top of the pie and sprinkle with chocolate shavings. Thaw in the fridge for 25 minutes or on the counter for 15 minutes, before serving.

Coconut Cream Pie

Preparation Time: 30 minutes / **Chilling Time:** 2 hours

Equipment: *One 12 x 18-inch baking sheet lined with parchment paper, a 9 or 10-inch pie plate or dish, a food processor fitted with a steel blade.*

I have to confess that I was never very keen on coconut cream pies, mostly because I was not that fond of the packaged, sweetened coconut, commonly found in the baking aisles of most grocery stores. Then one day, when I found that I had some time on my hands, I decided to buy a fresh coconut, drain the juice, hammer the shell off, and sweeten and toast the flesh of the coconut, myself. I did say that I had time on my hands. The result was life changing for my relationship with coconut. I had never tasted such delicious, crispy morsels of goodness. I realize that buying and cracking open a fresh coconut is not user friendly. So, I began the hunt for organic packaged coconut that still was fresh, free of additives and unsweetened. This I found in specialty stores such as Whole Foods and other health food stores. I still sweeten and toast the packaged organic coconut in the same way as I did with the fresh, and while not quite as good as a fresh shelled coconut, it still is very tasty.

SHORTCRUST PASTRY
(or you can use a store-bought pie crust)

2 cups flour

¾ cup butter, cubed and cold

1 tablespoon sugar

½ teaspoon salt

¼ cup water, cold

1 teaspoon pure vanilla extract

1 whisked egg white for brushing on the baked crust

GARNISH

1¼ cups whipping cream

¼ cup icing sugar

1 cup sweetened, toasted coconut

Fresh fruit such as peaches, nectarines, or mango slices

FILLING

1 tin, 1½ cups full fat coconut cream (found in the same aisle as coconut milk)

1½ cups whipping cream

5 egg yolks

½ cup sugar

¼ cup flour

1 teaspoon vanilla

2 tablespoons butter

¼ teaspoon salt

1 cup unsweetened organic coconut (sweetened and toasted, recipe follows)

SWEETENING & TOASTING THE COCONUT

Preheat the oven to 350°F. In a medium saucepan, combine ½ cup of water, ½ cup of sugar and 2 teaspoons of vanilla. Heat until all the sugar is dissolved. Add 2 cups of coconut and stir until the coconut is evenly coated with the syrup. Remove the coconut with a slotted spoon and spread out on a parchment lined baking sheet. Bake until the edges of the coconut become golden brown, about 7 minutes, stirring halfway through so that the coconut browns, evenly. Set aside. If you like a fine coconut and the coconut is in larger pieces you can give it a finer chop. You will add one cup to the filling and reserve one cup for the garnish.

PIE CRUST (Fully Blind-Baked)

Place the flour, sugar, and salt in the bowl of the food processor and pulse to combine. Add the butter to the flour and pulse until the butter is in large pea size pieces. Add the vanilla to the water, take the lid off the food processor, and dribble over the flour. Pulse briefly to incorporate the water but stop before the dough comes together completely. Scrape the dough out onto a large piece of floured parchment or wax paper. Knead a few times to bring the dough together. Form into a smooth disk, cover in plastic wrap and refrigerate for 1 hour. Roll the dough out into a circle one and a half inches larger than your pie dish. With the help of the rolling pin, lift the dough over the center of your dish. Gently press the dough into the bottom and up the sides of the pie plate. Fold the edges under and flute, if desired. Place in the freezer for 15 minutes before baking.

Preheat the oven to 400°F. Line the pastry with a piece of crumpled up parchment paper and fill to the rim with commercial pie weights or beans. Bake for 20 minutes. Carefully, remove the parchment paper and prick the crust all over with the tines of a fork. Place the crust back in the oven for approximately 15 to 20 minutes. The crust should be golden brown all over. Remove from the oven and set aside. Brush a whisked egg white over the bottom of the warm crust. This will help to prevent the crust from becoming soggy, when filled. Let the crust cool at room temperature for 15 minutes, before placing it in the refrigerator to cool completely.

Recipe continues on page 202

As you can see by the size of the coconut pieces, I made this the epic day of the fresh coconut shelling.

FILLING (this can be made a day or two ahead)

In a medium sized bowl, whisk the flour and egg yolks together. Pour the coconut cream and whipping cream into a heavy bottomed saucepan. Add the sugar and bring the cream/milk to a simmer. Remove from the heat and gradually add ½ cup of the hot cream to the yolk mixture, whisking to combine. Slowly add the rest of the hot cream to the yolks, continuing to whisk as you pour. Pour the custard mixture back into the saucepan and return the saucepan to a medium low heat.

Bring to a simmer, then to a boil very gradually. You will be whisking constantly throughout this process. When the mixture comes to a boil, allow to boil for 2 minutes. The custard should be thick and have a pudding-like consistency. Remove from the heat and whisk in the vanilla, salt, and butter. Strain the custard through a large-holed sieve into a heat proof bowl. Add 1 cup of the toasted coconut, stirring well to incorporate. The coconut pieces can be more finely chopped, if too large for your liking. Allow the custard to cool on the counter for 20 minutes, stirring only occasionally.

Place plastic wrap directly on the custard and refrigerate until cold. Fill the pie shell with the cold set custard.

GARNISH

Whip the cream with the sugar, until stiff peaks form. Cover the top of the pie generously with the whipped cream. Sprinkle the remaining coconut over the whipped cream. Garnish the pie with fresh fruit that goes well with coconut, such as nectarines, mangos, or peaches.

This pie can be refrigerated for 3 days or frozen, without the garnish, for up to 1 month. To freeze: place uncovered on a baking sheet in the freezer. When frozen, wrap in plastic wrap, then in aluminum foil.

Roasted Rhubarb & Strawberry Tray Bake

Preparation Time: 40 minutes / **Chilling Time:** 20 minutes / **Baking Time:** 30 minutes

Equipment: *One 8 x 14-inch baking tray with sides or brownie pan, a stand mixer fitted with the paddle attachment or handheld mixer.*

I love the yin and yang of rhubarb and strawberries, the tartness of the rhubarb and the sweetness of the strawberries balance each other so perfectly. I have marinated and roasted the fruit, rather than baking it, as roasting allows the fruit to maintain its shape and intensity of flavor. It also looks gorgeous. This tart consists of an easy to make shortbread crust and a no bake cream cheese filling. It is a perfect dessert to make in the Spring when both fruits are ripe and fragrant.

SHORTBREAD CRUST

1 cup butter at room temperature

½ cup icing sugar

1 teaspoon vanilla

2 cups flour, loosely scooped and leveled

½ teaspoon salt

FRUIT

2 pints of strawberries

8 stalks of rhubarb

½ cup maple syrup

2 tablespoons balsamic vinegar

2 tablespoons orange juice

2 teaspoons of orange zest

FILLING

2 bricks (500 grams) of cream cheese

½ cup sour cream

½ cup sugar

1 teaspoon vanilla

CRUST

Whisk together the flour and salt on a large piece of parchment paper. In the bowl of the stand mixer, cream the butter and sugar together until very light and fluffy, at least one minute. Add the vanilla. Tip in the flour and mix until just incorporated. Scrape the dough out onto a floured piece of parchment or wax paper. Knead a few times and then press the dough into your baking pan. Spread the dough evenly over the bottom and sides of the pan. I usually place clumps of dough in the corners and in the middle of the pan for easier spreading and use an offset spatula to even out the dough.

Recipe continues on the next page

Prick the dough all over with the tines of a fork and place in the freezer for 20 minutes.

Preheat the oven to 350°F. Bake for 18 to 20 minutes, until the crust is golden brown around the edges. Let cool at room temperature for 15 minutes, then place in the fridge or freezer to cool, completely.

FRUIT

Preheat the oven to 350°F. In a medium size saucepan, mix together the maple syrup, vinegar, orange juice and zest. Heat on medium high speed until the mixture comes to a low boil. Allow to boil for 5 minutes, until the mixture is reduced slightly in volume. This will concentrate the flavors. Set aside to cool.

Wash and dry the fruit. Halve the strawberries and cut the rhubarb into 1-inch pieces. Lightly toss the fruit in flour and place the fruit on a parchment lined baking tray. Separate the strawberries from the rhubarb as the strawberries will cook faster. Liberally brush the marinade all over the fruit. Roast the fruit for 7 minutes, remove from the oven and liberally brush once more with the marinade. Remove the strawberries and allow the rhubarb to cook for 5 more minutes. You want the fruit to be tender, but to hold their shape. Allow the fruit to cool completely at room temperature or in the refrigerator.

FILLING

In the bowl of the stand mixer, cream together the cream cheese, sugar, and vanilla. Add the sour cream and mix until smooth. Pour over the cold crust and smooth to the edges with an offset spatula. Allow the filling to set for at least 1 hour before adding the fruit.

ASSEMBLY

Place the fruit on top of the filling. I like to place the rhubarb and strawberries in their own rows for a pretty presentation. Garnish with whipped cream.

This tart can be refrigerated for 3 days, or frozen for up to 1 month. If freezing, freeze the cooled tart uncovered on a baking sheet. When frozen, wrap well in plastic wrap, then aluminum foil.

Summer Peach & Blueberry Galette

Preparation Time: 20 minutes / **Chilling Time:** 45 minutes / **Baking Time:** 40 minutes

Equipment: *One 12 x 18-inch cooking sheet lined with parchment paper, a food processor fitted with the steel blade.*

This is an easy fruit tart to make and it is a good late summer bake, when both fruits are readily available and at their peak. At one time I had blueberry bushes in my backyard. I had to pick them as soon as they were ripe, at first light, as I was in competition with the crows. The crows would swoop down and feast on them over a two-day period, until they were all gone.

SHORTCRUST PASTRY

2½ cups flour

1 cup cold butter, cubed

2 tablespoon sugar

¼ cold water with 1 teaspoon lemon juice added

½ teaspoon salt

Egg wash for crust (1 egg mixed with 2 teaspoon of water)

Turbinado or white sugar

FRUIT

A mixture of 4 cups of peaches and blueberries

4 tablespoons of sugar

1 tablespoon of lemon juice

2 tablespoons of flour

½ cup Apricot or peach jam, warmed

SHORTCRUST PASTRY

Place the flour, salt, and sugar in the bowl of the food processor. Pulse briefly to combine. Sprinkle the cold cubed butter over the flour and pulse in very short intervals until the butter is broken up into large pea size pieces. Lift the lid off the food processor and sprinkle the water and lemon juice over the flour. Pulse again just to incorporate the liquid. The mixture should look raggedy and somewhat dry at this point. Scrape the pastry dough out into a large mixing bowl or a floured piece of parchment paper. With floured hands, bring the dough together into a large disk. If the dough seems too dry, you can add another tablespoon of water. Wrap the disk in plastic wrap and refrigerate for 45 minutes. (You will only need ⅔ of the pastry for the galette so you can freeze the rest for later use.)

FILLING

Wash the fruit and place in a mixing bowl. Toss with the sugar, jam and lemon juice. Work the flour into the fruit lightly but well. You can use more sugar if the fruit is quite tart. Set aside.

ASSEMBLY

Preheat the oven to 350°F. Bring the pastry out of the fridge and let sit for 15 minutes before rolling. Roll into a circle approximately 12 inches in diameter. Leaving a border of 1½ inches, fill the circle generously with fruit. Bring the edges of the pastry up and over the fruit making pleats in the pastry, where necessary. Brush the pastry with the egg wash and sprinkle with sugar.

This tart will keep in the refrigerator for 3 days or can be frozen for up to 1 month. To freeze: place the cooled tart on a baking sheet in the freezer unwrapped. When frozen, wrap in plastic wrap, then in aluminum foil.

Goat Cheese Honey Roasted Fig Tart

Preparation Time: 40 minutes / **Chilling Time:** 4 hours or overnight

Equipment: *A stand mixer fitted with the whisk and paddle attachment, or handheld mixer, a 12 x 18-inch parchment lined baking sheet.*

This is a fairly easy tart to assemble and, to make it even easier, I have used a good quality store bought pie crust. The crust can be fully blind-baked ahead of time and frozen until you are ready to fill it. The roasted figs definitely are the star of this show, and the lightly whipped goat cheese filling provides a truly lovely backdrop for the sweetly scented fruit. I have had several requests for this recipe from people living in more temperate climates, who just happen to have their own fig trees. I can only imagine.

PIE CRUST

1 (9-inch) frozen pie crust, fully blind-baked
1 whisked egg white

ROASTED FIGS

8 fresh figs
½ cup honey
2 tablespoons brandy
½ cup white wine
¼ teaspoon cinnamon
½ teaspoon pure vanilla extract
A few sprigs of fresh thyme

GOAT CHEESE FILLING

1 block of cream cheese (250 grams)
1 cup or 250 grams of goat cheese
½ cup full fat sour cream
¼ cup sugar
¼ cup honey
2 teaspoons each of lemon zest and juice
Pinch of salt

GARNISH

White chocolate shavings, sprigs of rosemary and/or thyme and/or chopped pistachios

BLIND BAKING THE TART SHELL

Preheat the oven to 400°F. Thaw the frozen pie shell according to package instructions, but it should be cold, before baking. Crumple up a piece of parchment paper and line the tart shell. Fill the shell with commercial pie weights or dried beans. Bake for 20 minutes. Carefully, remove the parchment paper and prick the crust all over with the tines of a fork. Place the crust back in the oven to fully bake for another 15 minutes. The crust should be golden brown. Remove from the oven and set aside. Brush a whisked egg white over the bottom of the crust. This will help to prevent the crust from going soggy, when filled. Let the crust cool at room temperature for 15 minutes, before placing it in the refrigerator or freezer to cool completely.

ROASTING THE FIGS

Preheat the oven to 350°F. Combine the honey, brandy, wine, rosemary, thyme, vanilla, and cinnamon in a large measuring cup and warm in the microwave for 40 seconds. Give it a good stir. Cut the figs in half, brush the cut side of the figs with the marinade and place the figs cut side down on the prepared baking sheet. Pour the rest of the marinade over the figs. Bake the figs until tender but still holding their shape, basting the figs occasionally with the cooking syrup. This will take 15 to 20 minutes, depending on the ripeness of the figs. Remove from the oven and allow the figs to cool in their juices.

FILLING

Add the goat cheese and cream cheese to the bowl of the stand mixer and mix until smooth. Gradually add the sugar and honey and beat until fully incorporated. Add the sour cream, vanilla, lemon juice and zest. Pour the filling into the cold pie shell. Allow the filling to chill in the refrigerator, uncovered, for 2 hours. At this point, you can place the cut figs decoratively around the top of the tart. Loosely cover the tart and allow the tart to set for another 2 hours or overnight.

GARNISH

Just before serving, drizzle warm honey over the figs. Garnish with some sprigs of fresh thyme or chopped pistachios and/or shavings of white chocolate.

This tart keeps well in the refrigerator for 3 days or in the freezer for 1 month. To freeze: place cooled tart uncovered on a baking sheet. When frozen: wrap in plastic wrap, then in aluminum foil.

Profiteroles with Vanilla Pastry Cream & Chocolate Sauce

Preparation Time: 30 minutes / **Baking Time:** 30 minutes* / **Chilling Time:** 6 hours

Equipment: *A food processor fitted with a steel blade, two 12 x 18-inch baking sheets lined with parchment paper, one 16-inch piping bag with a large ½ inch with a plain round tip, or ½ inch opening, one 16-inch piping bag with a smaller round plain or star tip for filling with pastry cream.*

Profiteroles remind me of childhood trips to Quebec, where in one very special restaurant, our parents would allow us to choose a dessert from a pastry trolley. It always was a toss-up between the eclairs and the profiteroles. No matter which one I chose, I would always look over at the circulating cart and want the other! Profiteroles involve making a choux pastry. This is not difficult but requires paying close attention to the mixing directions. Once you have mastered choux pastry it opens the door to all kinds of sweet and savory treats, such as cheese puffs and, of course, eclairs.

CHOUX PASTRY

½ cup butter

½ cup water

½ cup milk

1 tablespoon sugar

1 cup all-purpose flour, scooped and leveled

4 large eggs, beaten

¼ teaspoon salt

Egg wash: 1 egg whisked with 2 teaspoons of water

VANILLA PASTRY CREAM

1½ cups milk

½ cup whipping cream

2 teaspoons vanilla bean paste or pure vanilla extract

¼ cup flour

6 egg yolks at room temperature

½ cup sugar

2 tablespoons butter

¼ teaspoon salt

CHOCOLATE SAUCE

See recipe for Chocolate Sauce
(page 252)

CHOUX PASTRY

Preheat the oven to 425°F. Combine the milk, water and butter in a medium heavy bottomed saucepan and place over medium high heat. When the butter has melted, take the saucepan off the heat and dump in the flour, all at once. Stir the flour mixture vigorously, turn the heat down to low and return the saucepan to the burner. Continue stirring vigorously for about 2 minutes. The flour mixture will begin to clump together and coat the bottom of the pan. Remove from the heat and scrape the mixture into the bowl of the food processor. Allow the dough to cool down for a few minutes. You can pulse the dough briefly 3 or 4 times in the food processor to help with the cooling process. Meanwhile, whisk your eggs together in a separate bowl. With the food processor running, add the eggs gradually, one at a time. This will prevent the eggs from scrambling. Pulse the pastry in short bursts until the mixture becomes smooth, thick, and glossy. This will take anywhere from 40 seconds to one minute.

Transfer the choux pastry to a large piping bag fitted with a ½ inch tip or simply cut a ½ inch opening at the end of the bag. Holding the piping bag directly above the mound you are about to pipe, pipe 2-inch mounds, 2 inches apart on the prepared baking sheet. I do about 9 profiteroles per tray. Pat down the peaks with a wet finger to make nice, round shapes. Brush each pastry lightly with egg wash. Bake one sheet at a time in the middle rack of the oven.

After 15 minutes, turn down the heat to 360°F. Bake for another 10 to 15 minutes. The profiteroles should be nicely browned and crisp looking. Transfer to a rack to cool before filling with the pastry cream.

VANILLA PASTRY CREAM* (can be made 2 days ahead)

In a medium size bowl, whisk the egg yolks together then add the sugar. Mix until just incorporated. Heat the milk and cream in a medium saucepan until it reaches a simmer. Do not boil. Remove from the heat and slowly stream in ½ cup of the hot milk into the egg mixture, whisking as you go. This will temper the eggs so that they will not scramble. Next, add the flour, whisking until there are no lumps. Gradually stream in the rest of the hot milk/cream, still whisking as you go, before returning the pastry cream to the saucepan.

Heat over medium low heat, whisking constantly, until the mixture begins to boil. Boil for 1 minute, stirring vigorously, then take off the heat and add the vanilla paste or extract, salt and butter. Return to the heat and, still whisking vigorously, boil for 1 more minute. The mixture should be thick like pudding at this point. Strain the cream through a large-holed sieve into a heat proof container. Allow to cool on the counter for 30 minutes, stirring only occasionally. Then place plastic wrap directly on top of the pastry cream to prevent a skin from forming and refrigerate until cold. It is best to leave the pastry cream to firm up for 6 hours or overnight.

CHOCOLATE SAUCE

Prepare according to chocolate sauce recipe on page 252.

ASSEMBLY

Fill a pastry bag fitted with a round tip with the cold pastry cream. Make a small "X" with a sharp knife in the bottom of the pastry and fill the puff until the pressure lets you know the puff is full of cream. Generously, pour the cooled chocolate sauce over each profiterole.

Profiteroles will keep in airtight containers in the fridge for 3 days or can be frozen for up to 2 months. Freeze the profiteroles, unwrapped on the baking sheets. Once frozen, cover with wax paper and place in airtight containers.

Pear Tarte Tatin

Preparation Time: 20 minutes / **Baking Time:** 25 minutes

Equipment: *A 9 or 10-inch cast iron skillet or stove to oven skillet.*

A traditional French recipe, tarte tatin often is made with apples, which are caramelized in sugar in a cast iron skillet. Puff pastry is placed over the sauteed fruit, and the skillet is placed in the oven to finish cooking. When plated, the skillet is turned upside down showing the caramelized fruit on the top. I have chosen Bosc pears for the fruit as they still are a hardy fruit, make for a wonderful presentation and are simply lovely paired with caramel and cinnamon. However, if you love apples or have an abundance feel free to substitute.

Frozen Butter Puff Pastry (thawed according to instructions), but cold when used

4 to 5 medium to large sized firm Bosc pears

1 cup sugar

¼ cup water

1 teaspoon vanilla

½ teaspoon cinnamon

2 tablespoons cold butter

Pinch of salt

Preheat the oven to 400°F. Slice the pears in half, peel, and core. Then slice each half of the pear into thirds, leaving one half of a pear for the center of the tart. Place one cup of sugar in the skillet. Carefully pour ¼ of water over the sugar, being careful not to splash the sides. Bring to a boil, stirring occasionally. When the mixture turns into a rich amber color, take the skillet off the stove and add the butter, vanilla, cinnamon and salt.

Carefully arrange the pear slices in the caramel, placing the ½ pear in the center core side up. The caramel will be very hot. Return the saucepan to a medium high heat. Let the caramel simmer around the pears for another 5 minutes and be sure to spoon some of the caramel over the pears so that they are evenly coated. Take the skillet off the heat.

Bring the puff pastry out of the fridge and, between 2 sheets of waxed paper, roll the pastry into a 12-inch circle. With the help of your floured rolling pin, lift the pastry over the center of the skillet. Using a knife or offset spatula, gently tuck the pastry in and around the pears. Place the skillet in the oven until the pastry is nicely browned, approximately 20 to 25 minutes. Allow to cool for 10 minutes, then turn the tart out onto a clean plate or serving dish.

Tarte Tatin keeps well in the fridge for 3 days and is delicious served warm with ice cream. It freezes well for up to 1 month. To freeze: place cooled tart unwrapped on a baking sheet in the freezer. When frozen, cover in plastic wrap, then in aluminum foil.

Mille Feuille or Napoleon's

Preparation Time: 1 hour / **Baking Time:** 30 minutes / **Chilling Time:** 6 hours

Equipment: *Four 12 x 18-inch baking sheets, lined with parchment paper, kitchen scissors or a sharp knife to trim the puff pastry, a stand mixer fitted with the whisk attachment or handheld mixer, 2 large piping bags fitted with ½ inch star tip or simply cut open, 1 small piping bag with ¼ inch opening for applying the glaze.*

Biting into crunchy layers of pastry (*mille feuille* means a thousand layers) filled with pastry cream or fresh whipped cream, just is bliss in a bite. In this recipe, I have used a good quality store bought butter puff pastry. I also have made two fillings, one a stabilized whipped cream with raspberries and the other a traditional vanilla pastry cream, which is used in the Profiterole recipe. Feel free to make only one filling, they are both fantastic. Most bakeries use gelatin to keep their whipped cream fresh and I have used it, here. It is a very handy tip to know especially because it allows you to make a whipped cream dessert well in advance of a dinner party.

MILLE FEUILLE PASTRY

1 package of frozen butter puff pastry, thawed according to instructions, but cold when used (one box of pastry with 2 sheets will make 6 to 8 mille feuilles)

VANILLA PASTRY CREAM

1 batch of Vanilla Pastry Cream (see pastry cream recipe under Profiteroles, page 212)

STABILIZED WHIPPED CREAM WITH RASPBERRIES

2 cups whipping cream

½ cup icing sugar

1 packet of gelatin (2½ teaspoons)

3 tablespoons of water

1 pint of raspberries (chopped in half)

GLAZE

3 cups icing sugar

¼ cup milk

2 teaspoons vanilla

¼ cup unsweetened cocoa powder

MILLE FEUILLE PUFF PASTRY

Lightly roll out 1 sheet of puff pastry on a floured piece of parchment or wax paper into a rectangle, only slightly larger than its original size. Leave the rest of the puff pastry in the refrigerator until ready to use. Using a ruler as a guide and with kitchen scissors, cut out rectangles, approximately 2 x 5 inches. You will need 3 rectangles to make one mille feuille. Place the rectangles on parchment lined baking sheets, about 1½ inches apart. Dock each rectangle with the tines of a fork. When you finish filling the baking sheets, cover each sheet of rectangles with a sheet of crumpled parchment paper. Then, fit a same sized baking sheet over the parchment paper, bottom side down, and refrigerate the covered baking sheets for 20 minutes.

Preheat the oven to 400°F. Bake the pastry, one sheet at a time, still covered with a baking sheet, in the middle rack of the oven. The top baking sheet will keep the rectangles flat, while baking. Bake for 15 minutes, then remove the baking sheet and parchment paper and bake for 15 minutes more, until the pastry is a lovely golden brown. I turn the pastry over near the end of the baking time to ensure a crunchy bottom pastry, but this will depend on your oven. It is not necessary. Set aside to cool and continue baking the rest of the rectangles.

PASTRY CREAM

See Pastry Cream Instructions under Profiteroles (page 212).

STABILIZED WHIPPED CREAM

Place 3 tablespoons of cool water in a cereal sized microwavable bowl and sprinkle one packet of gelatin over the water. Stir to combine and allow the gelatin to bloom for 5 minutes. After 5 minutes, microwave the gelatin for 10 seconds, then 5 seconds until the gelatin becomes liquid. Gelatin cannot be boiled so be careful not to over-heat. The gelatin should feel smooth, not grainy to the touch.

Pour the whipping cream into the bowl of the stand mixer. Beat on medium high speed, gradually adding the sugar and vanilla as the cream thickens. When the cream just begins to form stiff peaks, it is time to add the gelatin. Take out ½ cup of whipped cream and add it to the melted gelatin. Mix well. Then add the whipped cream and gelatin mixture back into the rest of the whipped cream. Continue beating until stiff peaks form. Remove the bowl from the stand and fold in the chopped raspberries.

Recipe continues on the next page

GLAZE

Place the icing sugar in a mixing bowl. Add the vanilla to the milk and warm up the milk in the microwave for 20 seconds. Pour all but 1 tablespoon of the milk over the icing sugar, whisking until you have a smooth glaze. You want a thick, but spreadable glaze, so that it does not drip over the sides of the mille feuille. Transfer ½ cup of the glaze to a small bowl and sift in the cocoa powder. Add the reserved tablespoon of warm milk to the cocoa glaze and whisk until smooth.

ASSEMBLY

The top layer of each mille feuille will be spread with the glaze and you can prepare the top layers, before assembling the rest of the layers. With an offset spatula, spread the white glaze over each of the top rectangles of pastry. Place the cocoa glaze in a small piping bag and pipe 5 to 7 stripes of chocolate glaze widthwise across each one. Using a toothpick or a knife blade, drag the tip lengthwise down the lines of chocolate going first in one direction and then in the opposite direction to make a chevron pattern. Set aside to dry.

I used a 16-inch piping bag fitted with a large star tip to pipe the fillings, but you can simply spread the filling with an offset spatula or spoon. Pipe or spread the bottom layer of pastry evenly with pastry cream, then top with a second rectangle. Pipe or spread the raspberry whipped cream over this rectangle. Top with the glazed rectangle. The mille feuilles will keep in an airtight container in the fridge for 3 days or can be frozen for up to 1 month. To freeze: place uncovered on a baking sheet in the freezer. When frozen, place in an airtight container with a layer of wax paper over the pastries.

Desserts
For A Crowd

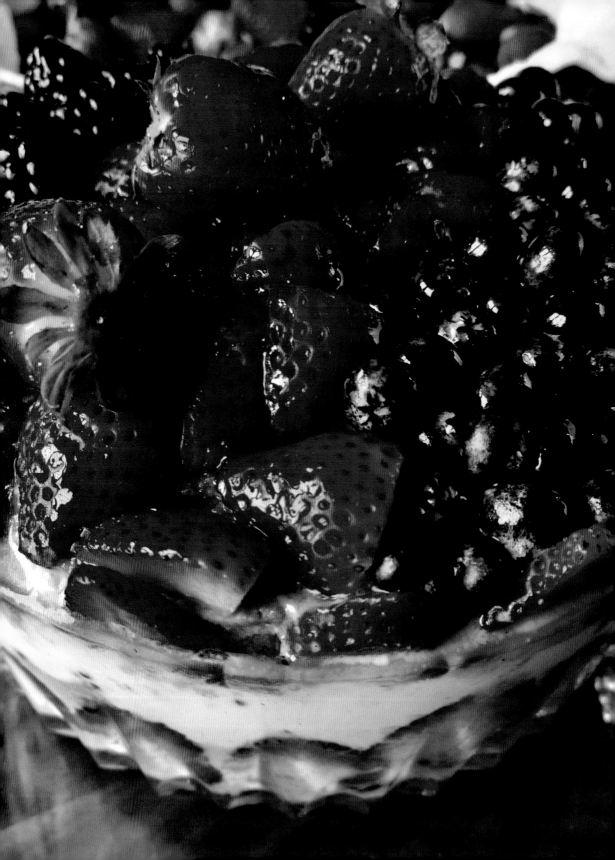

Nana's British Berry Trifle

Preparation Time: 1 hour / **Chilling Time:** 2 hours or overnight

Equipment: *A stand mixer with the whisk attachment or handheld mixer, a large glass bowl.*

Trifle is all about the layering of fruit, cake, custard and/or cream and you really can't go wrong no matter how you do this. Nana usually bought a lemon pound cake, sliced it and smothered the slices in a good raspberry jam. She always used Bird's custard and mostly followed the directions on the can. However, she added slightly more powder than called for to make the custard less runny and, when it was finished cooking, two dollops of butter, brandy and some vanilla extract were added as well. Nana loved her butter (and her brandy) and I think this was a carryover from experiencing rationing in England, during the war years. The result of Nana's efforts was a magnificent dessert, not only beautiful to look at and deliciously satisfying, but also a memory in the making of Nana and the family get-togethers for which the trifle was made.

FRUIT

4 pints of berries of your choice
(a mix of strawberries, raspberries,
blueberries, or blackberries is nice
for color)
¼ to ½ cup sugar
1 tablespoon lemon juice

CUSTARD

⅓ cup Bird's Hill custard powder
2 cups whole milk
½ cup whipping cream
⅓ cup sugar
2 tablespoons butter
2 teaspoons vanilla extract
1 tablespoon brandy (optional)
¼ teaspoon salt

WHIPPED CREAM LAYER

2 cups whipping cream
½ cup icing sugar
2 teaspoons vanilla extract

CAKE

1 vanilla or lemon pound cake cut into
½ inch thick slices (you will need
enough for two layers)
½ cup good raspberry or strawberry jam

MAKE THE CUSTARD

Combine the milk and cream and warm in the microwave for one minute. In a large saucepan, mix together ⅓ cup of Bird's custard with ⅓ cup sugar. Gradually add ½ cup of the warm milk/cream mixture until a smooth paste is made. I use a wooden spoon and make sure to scrape around the bottom edges of the pan, where I find the custard powder tends to stick. Place the saucepan over medium heat and gradually whisk in the rest of the milk/cream. Bring the custard to a low boil, whisking constantly. Allow the custard to boil for 2 minutes before taking it off the heat. Add the butter, salt, brandy, if using, and vanilla. Pour into a large bowl (for quicker cooling) and let cool at room temperature for 20 minutes, stirring occasionally. Place plastic wrap directly over the custard and refrigerate until cold. The custard can be made 1 or 2 days in advance.

FRUIT

Wash the fruit and slice the strawberries. Reserve 6 to 8 whole strawberries for garnish. Place the berries in a large bowl and sprinkle the sugar and the lemon juice over them. Mix well and let the fruit sit for 30 minutes. This will macerate the fruit and intensify their flavor.

WHIPPED CREAM

In the bowl of the stand mixer, fitted with the whisk attachment or with a handheld mixer, beat the whipping cream. As the cream thickens, gradually add the icing sugar and the vanilla extract. Beat until stiff peaks form. Set aside.

ASSEMBLY

Warm the raspberry jam for easy spreading for about 30 seconds in the microwave. Cut the pound cake into ½ inch slices. You will need enough for two layers. Spread the warm raspberry jam on the slices.

Place some berries on the bottom of the trifle bowl and cover them with custard. Assemble a layer of cake over the custard. Liberally layer more berries over the cake and once again cover with custard. Top with the second cake layer. Cover this layer liberally with berries and top with a thick layer of whipped cream. Place fruit attractively on top of the cream. Decorate the top with a few whole strawberries. Mint leaves also look nice. Place any leftover custard in a pitcher, add 2 more tablespoons of brandy (optional) and serve it warm over the portions of trifle, or let the guests help themselves.

Vintage Baked Alaska

Preparation Time: 1 hour / **Freezing Time:** 8 hours, or overnight

Equipment: *1 round 8 or 9-inch medium to large size bowl, buttered or sprayed with oil, covered in 2 or 3 layers of plastic wrap with a 2-inch overhang for easy removal, a stand mixer fitted with the whisk attachment or handheld mixer.*

There is something so exotic looking about a baked Alaska. I vaguely remember my parents going to a dinner party and talking about having this wonderful ice cream dessert covered in meringue. One Saturday morning, I was thinking about what to make for a family reunion and the idea of a Baked Alaska took hold. This dessert really does feed a crowd of up to 20 people. The best thing about it, though, is you get to choose the flavors of ice-cream that you like the most. In this case, I used raspberry, vanilla, and chocolate, but any combination will do. Note: This dessert is easily made gluten-free by omitting the base cake layer.

1 store bought chocolate or marble pound cake or round sponge cake layer

3 pints of ice cream of your choice (I chose chocolate, raspberry and vanilla)

8 egg whites at room temperature or 1 cup of pasteurized egg whites found in a carton in most grocery stores (if you are worried about uncooked egg whites, use the carton, the meringue is cooked, but briefly)

1 cup sugar

½ teaspoon cream of tartar

1 teaspoon pure vanilla extract

ICE CREAM

Allow the ice cream to sit out on the counter for 10 minutes. Scoop the ice cream in contrasting colors into the prepared bowl. Make sure there are no gaps between the flavors. Cut the pound cake into ½ inch slices and press the cake lightly onto the ice cream, at the top of the bowl. This will be your base when you invert the bowl. Wrap the open end of the bowl with plastic wrap and place in the freezer for 8 hours or overnight. Bring the bowl out of the freezer 5 minutes before you plan to make the meringue topping.

Recipe continues on page 227

MERINGUE

Preheat the oven to 450°F. Place the egg whites in a heat proof bowl over a pan of simmering water. There should be no more than two inches of water in the pan. Gradually add the sugar to the whites, whisking constantly. When the egg whites are foamy and feel warm to the touch, transfer them to the bowl of the stand mixer. Add the cream of tartar and vanilla and beat the egg whites on high speed until stiff peaks form.

Unmold the ice cream onto a baking sheet lined with parchment paper, peeling back the layers of plastic wrap. If the ice cream does not unmold readily, place the bowl in a pan of shallow hot water for one minute and try again. Generously spoon the meringue over the ice cream and make decorative swirls in the meringue with the spoon. You can also pipe the meringue using a piping bag and a large star tip. Place the Alaska on the top rack of the oven and bake for 4 or 5 minutes or until the meringue is lightly browned. Remove. If the meringue has gaps in the browning, you can use a small kitchen blow torch to toast the meringue in places that were missed. Note: Alternatively, you can avoid the oven, altogether, and use the blow torch, only, to toast the meringue.

Place the Baked Alaska back in the freezer, uncovered, until ready to serve. Allow the Alaska to sit at room temperature for at least 10 minutes, before serving, then use a sharp serrated knife to cut thin slices. If not serving right away, allow the Alaska to sit in the freezer uncovered for one hour, then wrap in plastic wrap and cover with aluminum foil. The Alaska will keep frozen for two weeks.

Cherries Jubilee

(GLUTEN-FREE)

Preparation Time: 20 minutes

Equipment: *One 9 or 10-inch skillet, glass dishes or wine glasses for serving, a long lighter.*

There were five children in our family, and, like many families of our time, we rarely went out to a restaurant to eat. If we did, it was to the Cozy Corner restaurant for fish and chips. On the day I graduated from university, I was taken to a very fancy restaurant in Toronto, called Julie's. It was there that I first experienced this most impressive dessert, which came to the table alight in tall flames. It was a moment that I will never forget. This dessert is so easy to make that I wonder why I let all these years pass without sharing it with my guests.

1 quart of good quality vanilla ice cream

1 pound of fresh bing cherries or canned bing cherries

½ cup orange juice

½ cup sugar

2 tablespoons cornstarch

Zest of 1 orange

⅓ cup brandy

Wash and pit the cherries. (You can buy a small plastic cherry pitter very cheaply at hardware stores.)

In a small bowl, mix ¼ cup of the orange juice with the cornstarch until a thick paste forms. Place the rest of the juice, zest and sugar in a large deep skillet and heat over medium high heat, until the sugar is dissolved. Add the cornstarch paste and allow the mixture to boil, whisking until thickened. Add the cherries and allow the cherries to simmer in the juice for 5 minutes. While the cherries are cooking, scoop the ice cream into serving dishes or wine glasses and place on the table. Pour the brandy into the simmering sauce and quickly ignite the contents with a long lighter. Immediately bring the flaming skillet to the table and scoop the lit cherries over the ice cream.

Tipsy Tiramisu

Preparation Time: 20 minutes / No Bake / **Chilling Time:** 4 hours

Equipment: *One 13 x 9-inch casserole dish, preferably glass, or 8 smaller glass dishes, a stand mixer fitted with the whisk attachment or a handheld mixer.*

Tiramisu means "cheer me up" or "pick me up" according to different linguists. Both meanings make sense as the dessert is made with strong coffee, which is a definite pick me up, and your choice of brandy, sweet wine, or rum the likes of which always are cheering. I use egg yolks in this recipe whisked over a double boiler in the same way as one would make a sabayon. However, if you dislike the idea of making a no bake dessert with egg yolks, I have included a version of tiramisu that is eggless.

6 large egg yolks

3/4 cup superfine sugar, divided,
   1/2 cup for the egg yolks,
   2 tablespoons for whipping
   the cream and 2 tablespoons
   for the coffee syrup

2 cups mascarpone cheese at
   room temperature

1 block of cream cheese
   (250 grams)

¼ teaspoon salt

2 cups whipping cream

2 teaspoons pure vanilla extract

6 tablespoons rum divided
   (3 tablespoon for the coffee,
   3 tablespoon for the cheese
   filling)

1½ cups strong brewed
   espresso or regular brewed
   coffee

¼ cup unsweetened cocoa
   powder

40 to 48 crunchy style
   ladyfingers (I used Vicenzovo)

Combine the coffee with 2 tablespoons of sugar and 3 tablespoons of rum. Simmer over medium heat for three to five minutes until the sugar has dissolved and the coffee has reduced slightly. Set aside to cool.

Whisk the egg yolks in a heatproof bowl over a saucepan of simmering water. There should be no more than 2 inches of water in the saucepan. Gradually add ½ cup of sugar to the yolks, whisking constantly. Keep whisking the egg yolks until the yolks have thickened and lightened in color. This will take about 7 minutes. If the yolks get too hot, simply take them off the heat for a few seconds, then continue to whisk over the heat again. Set aside.

In the bowl of the stand mixer, beat the whipping cream. As the cream begins to thicken, add 2 tablespoons of sugar and the vanilla extract. Continue beating until the cream forms stiff peaks. Remove the whipping cream to a clean bowl.

Clean out the bowl of the mixer and the whisk and add the mascarpone and cream cheese. Whisk until smooth. Pour the thickened egg yolks into the cheese mixture and whisk until well incorporated. Add in the salt and remaining 3 tablespoons of rum. Then, fold the whipping cream into the cheese mixture, one third at a time.

ASSEMBLY

Dip the lady fingers into the cooled coffee. This should be a brief dip, on both sides, no longer than 2 seconds or the biscuits will disintegrate. Arrange the ladyfingers in a single layer in the prepared dish or in individual dishes, if using. Spread half of the cheese mixture over the cookies. Once again dip the lady fingers briefly in the coffee on both sides and arrange over the cheese layer. Spread the rest of the cheese over the lady fingers. Depending on the size of your pan, you might be able to do three layers of ladyfingers and cheese. Sprinkle the top with a good layer of cocoa powder. Refrigerate for at least 4 hours, or overnight, before serving.

EGGLESS TIRAMISU

Omit the egg yolks and whisk 1½ cups of room temperature mascarpone cheese with 1 cup of strained fine curd ricotta cheese. Blend in ¾ cup sugar, vanilla, rum and ¼ teaspoon of salt. You can do this by hand or use a stand mixer. Make the whipped cream as above and fold the cream by thirds into the cheese mixture. Proceed with the assembly as above.

Celestial Frozen Lemon Mousse Charlotte

Preparation Time: 20 minutes / **Chilling Time:** Overnight

Equipment: *One 10-inch springform pan, buttered and bottom lined with parchment paper, a stand mixer fitted with the whisk attachment or handheld mixer.*

I love lemon desserts and my favorite two are lemon tart and this frozen heavenly lemon mousse Charlotte. It feeds a crowd, and everyone loves the presentation. The mousse is surrounded by crunchy light lady fingers, and they become a unique form of cutlery as the guests inevitably use them to scoop up every bit of the melting mousse on their plates.

LEMON CURD

8 egg yolks at room temperature
½ cup butter
⅔ cup lemon juice (5 large lemons)
1¼ cups sugar
1 tablespoon lemon zest
Pinch of salt

WHIPPED CREAM

2 cups of cold whipping cream
½ cup of sugar
2 teaspoons of vanilla extract

LADY FINGERS

Approximately 45 to 50 lady fingers
  (I used Vicenzovo)
½ cup apricot or peach jam, warmed,
  to bind the lady fingers together

GARNISH

Fresh berries

LEMON CURD

In a medium sized saucepan, whisk the yolks together and add the sugar. Heat the lemon juice, zest and pinch of salt in the microwave for 30 seconds until lukewarm. Gradually, whisk the lemon juice into the yolks. Place the saucepan on a medium low heat and continue whisking the lemon mixture, until the mixture thickens, about 7 to 10 minutes. Do not let the lemon curd boil. To test if the curd is thick enough, dip in a wooden spoon and draw a finger across the back of the spoon. It should leave a trail. Take the curd off the heat and whisk in the butter. Let cool at room temperature for 15 minutes, stirring only occasionally. Then, place plastic wrap directly onto the curd and refrigerate until cold. If using on the same day, place the curd in the freezer. Note: The lemon curd can be made up to 3 days ahead of time.

WHIPPED CREAM

Add the whipping cream to the bowl of the stand mixer. Beat on medium high speed until the cream begins to thicken. Gradually add the sugar and continue beating on high speed until stiff peaks form. Add the vanilla and beat just until combined. Fold the whipped cream into the cold lemon curd. Set aside in the fridge while you assemble the lady fingers.

ASSEMBLY

Place the jam in a microwave bowl and warm for 25 seconds. Trim the ladyfingers to fit the sides of your pan. Dip one side of each trimmed ladyfinger in the jam so that it will adhere to the next ladyfinger as you line the springform pan. Place the ladyfingers in the pan trimmed end down and curved end on the outside to make for a pretty presentation. Fill the springform pan with the cold lemon mousse and smooth the top with an offset spatula. Place in the freezer uncovered until frozen. When frozen, cover with plastic wrap.

To serve: garnish with whipped cream, lemon slices and fresh berries. This dessert will keep well in the freezer for up to three weeks and serves up to 20 people.

Irish Whiskey Brioche Pudding with Whiskey Caramel Sauce

Preparation Time: 1 hour / **Baking Time:** 55 minutes

Equipment: *A 9 x 13-inch baking dish, buttered.*

This is a terrific morning after dish for guests. The pudding is good just on its own, but when you add a pitcher filled with a whiskey-enriched caramel sauce, it takes it over the top. It begins with day-old brioche or egg bread, which is then transformed by a creamy vanilla custard into an amazing brunch dish. There are never any leftovers and I swear I once saw a guest drinking the caramel sauce straight from the pitcher.

BREAD PUDDING

1 large loaf of day-old Brioche or Egg bread cut into cubes

¼ cup butter (melted)

3¼ cups whole milk

½ cup raisins

½ cup finely chopped dried apricots (optional)

3 tablespoons Irish Whiskey

4 eggs, room temperature

2 egg yolks, room temperature

½ cup dark brown sugar

½ cup white sugar

2 teaspoons vanilla extract

¼ teaspoon nutmeg

½ teaspoon cinnamon

TOP UP

1 cup whipping cream, whisked with 1 egg yolk and 2 tablespoons of Irish whiskey, to be added in the last 15 minutes of cooking time

Whiskey Caramel Sauce (see recipe on page 250)

BREAD PUDDING

Preheat the oven to 350°F. In a small saucepan, combine the raisins and apricots, if using. Add the whiskey and simmer over medium heat for 2 or 3 minutes. Set aside for the fruit to absorb most of the alcohol. Spread the cubes of bread evenly over the bottom of the baking dish. With a pastry brush, brush the bread with the melted butter. Place in the oven to crisp up for 5 to 7 minutes. Be careful not to burn the bread. Turn the oven off.

In a large bowl, whisk together the eggs, yolks and both sugars. Set aside. In a large saucepan, bring the milk to a simmer. Whisk ½ cup of hot milk into the eggs. Gradually add the rest of the milk, whisking constantly. Stir in the vanilla, nutmeg, and cinnamon. Scatter the fruit and any remaining whiskey over the bread cubes. Pour the custard mixture over the bread. Cover the bread pudding with plastic wrap and press down with your hands to ensure that all the bread has been soaked with the custard. Let sit for one hour. **Preheat the oven to 350°F.**

Place the bread pudding baking dish inside a much larger baking pan, lined with a tea towel. Pour boiling water into the larger pan until it reaches halfway up the baking dish. Bake for 40 minutes. Take the pans out of the oven and pour 1 cup of whipping cream, whisked with 1 egg yolk and 2 tablespoons of Irish whiskey, over the bread pudding. Place the pudding back in the oven and bake for 15 to 20 minutes more, until the cream has been all but absorbed and the pudding is golden brown. Serve warm with a pitcher of caramel sauce.

This dessert can be refrigerated for 4 days or frozen for up to 1 month. To freeze: place cooled bread pudding on a baking sheet, unwrapped. When frozen, wrap in plastic wrap, then in aluminum foil. To serve, thaw and rewarm.

White Chocolate Strawberry Celebration Cake

Preparation Time: 45 minutes / **Baking Time:** 15 minutes

Equipment: *A 12 x 18-inch rimmed cookie sheet, buttered and lined with parchment, a stand mixer fitted with the whisk attachment or handheld mixer.*

This is a perfect celebration cake for any occasion. It is fresh, sumptuous, and eye-catching. It is made with a genoise cake batter, the identical batter used in Mango Cakes on Fire. The combination of white chocolate, cream and strawberries simply is paradise on a plate. I served this at my daughter's graduation party, where there were at least 20 young people, and there was not a crumb left on the platter.

One 18 x 12-inch slab of vanilla genoise cake (see recipe for Mango Cakelets on Fire, page 152)

ORANGE SIMPLE SYRUP

See recipe under Mango Cakelets on Fire (page 152)

WHITE CHOCOLATE STRAWBERRY CREAM

1½ cups chopped white chocolate or three 100-gram bars

⅔ cup whipping cream (to be added to the chocolate)

2 cups whipping cream

¼ cup skim milk powder

½ cup icing sugar

2 cups washed and dried fresh strawberries

GARNISH

1 good quality white chocolate bar, shaved

Whole strawberries

Simple Syrup

CAKE

Make the cake according to the instructions for Mango Cakelets on Fire (page 152). Allow the cake to cool for 5 minutes. Cut a piece of parchment paper slightly larger than your rimmed cookie sheet and sprinkle it with icing sugar. Invert the cake onto the parchment paper and gently remove the parchment from the back of the cake. This will be a 3-layer cake. When completely cool, cut the cake layer width wise into three equal pieces. I use a pair of scissors and a ruler and make a 2-inch cut as a guide to where I will be making the 3 sections. While the cake is slightly warm, brush each of the 3 layers with the orange simple syrup.

WHITE CHOCOLATE STRAWBERRY CREAM

Melt the white chocolate in a heat proof bowl over simmering water. Warm up the whipping cream in the microwave for 45 seconds (it should be hot but not boiling) and add it to the melted chocolate, stirring until the chocolate is smooth. Allow the mixture to cool in the fridge, stirring every few minutes to make sure the chocolate does not harden.

Place two cups of whipping cream in the bowl of the stand mixer. Add the powdered milk, stirring to incorporate the powder. Beat on medium high speed until the cream begins to thicken. Add the icing sugar gradually and continue whisking at high speed until soft peaks begin to form. Add the vanilla and mix just until incorporated. When the chocolate has cooled enough that it will not melt the cream, scrape it into the mixing bowl and continue mixing on high speed until stiff peaks form. Set aside.

Chop the strawberries into ⅓ inch pieces, leaving a few of the nicest looking strawberries for garnish. Gently fold the strawberries into the whipped cream.

ASSEMBLY

Place one of the layers on a cake board or cutting board and cover the top with the strawberry cream. Repeat with the second and third layers. Garnish the top with shaved white chocolate and whole strawberries.

This cake will keep in the refrigerator for 3 days and can be frozen (without the garnish) for up to 1 month.

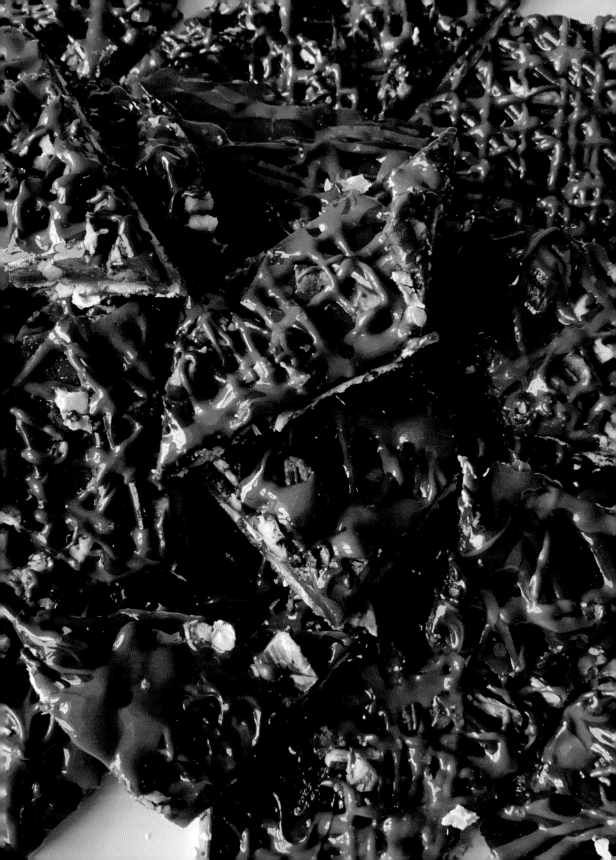

Toffee Pecan Crunch

Preparation Time: 15 minutes / **Baking Time:** 6 minutes

Equipment: *1 medium size cookie sheet (approximately 10 x 14-inch) lined with parchment paper.*

These simple-to-make sweets are my go-to for a crunchy, salty ever popular snack to fill out dessert platters. The base of the crunch is made with Saltines and who knew a simple cracker could be elevated to this level. Often made for the Christmas holidays, this toffee crunch is so addictively delicious that they have been given the nickname, "Christmas Crack."

1 cup toasted pecans
(baked at 350°F for about
6 to 7 minutes)

40 soda crackers (I used Saltines)

1 cup butter

1 cup dark brown sugar

1 teaspoon salt

GARNISH

1 cup dark 54% Callebaut chocolate
callets or Chipits

1 cup milk chocolate Callebaut
chocolate callets or Chipits

½ teaspoon coarse sea salt

Preheat the oven to 400°F. Line the saltines in a single layer on the prepared baking sheet. They should be touching but not overlapping. In a medium saucepan, melt the butter and add the brown sugar and salt. Bring to a boil and boil for about 4 minutes, stirring constantly, until the mixture becomes thick and amber brown in color. Pour the mixture carefully over the crackers. It is okay if the mixture does not completely cover all the crackers as the toffee will spread, when baked. Sprinkle the toasted pecans on top of the toffee.

Bake for 6 to 7 minutes or until you see that the toffee is bubbling. Cool for 20 minutes.

Place each of the chocolates in a microwaveable glass or dish. Microwave at 25 second intervals, stirring in between. Make sure to remove the chocolate as soon as the chocolate is fully melted, or it will seize. Drizzle the chocolate over the crackers. I use a piping bag, but you can use a spoon or a fork. Sprinkle coarse sea salt over the chocolate. These crackers can be kept in airtight containers in the cupboard for one week or can be frozen for up to one month.

Salted Caramels Dipped in Chocolate

Preparation Time: 30 minutes / **Chilling Time:** Overnight

Equipment: *A 13 x 9-inch pan lined with parchment paper and buttered, a slotted dipping fork, a heavy bottomed saucepan, a digital read thermometer.*

This confection is without a doubt the perfect party closer. Whether wrapped up in pretty tissue to take away as a party favor or presented as an after dinner treat, these chocolate covered caramels are a huge hit with guests. The caramel is wonderfully rich and has just the right amount of chew. You will need a digital read thermometer to make this confection.

1 cup butter

2½ cups dark brown sugar

¼ teaspoon salt

1 cup corn syrup

1 14-ounce can of sweetened
    condensed milk

1 tablespoon pure vanilla extract

DIPPING CHOCOLATE

2 cups Callebaut dark chocolate
    callets or chopped good quality
    chocolate and/or

2 cups Callebaut milk chocolate
    callets or chopped good quality
    chocolate

Coarse sea salt for sprinkling

In a medium to large saucepan, melt the butter. Add the rest of the ingredients, with the exception of the vanilla, and heat on medium high heat, stirring constantly, until the mixture is smooth and glossy. Bring the mixture to a boil and turn down the heat to medium. Continue to cook the caramel, stirring all the while, until the thermometer reads 248°F. This should take about 20 minutes. Do not rush this process or you may have to contend with a burnt pan. At the correct temperature, the caramel should be thick and have a rich tawny color.

Remove from the heat and add the vanilla, stirring until incorporated. Immediately pour the caramel into the prepared pan. Allow to cool for one hour at room temperature, then refrigerate overnight. The next day cut the caramels into one-inch pieces.

CHOCOLATE

Note: I like to dip half the caramels in milk chocolate and half in dark chocolate, but feel free to choose either/or. I also garnish some of the caramels with freshly toasted coconut and you can be as creative as you like with additions such as chopped nuts or cocoa powder.

Melt the chocolate in a heat proof bowl over a pan of simmering water. There should be no more than 2 inches of water in the pan. As the chocolate begins to melt, stir constantly. When the chocolate is warm and smooth (a digital read thermometer will register 32°C or 90°F) remove the bowl to a tea towel.

Begin to dip your caramels. Have a parchment lined baking sheet close at hand to receive the chocolate covered caramels. Simply drop the caramels in the chocolate, one at a time, and fetch them out with a long slotted fork, allowing the excess chocolate to drip off the fork back into the bowl. Before the chocolate sets, sprinkle the caramels with coarse sea salt.

These caramels will keep on the shelf for 2 weeks or can be refrigerated for up to three weeks.

Sheila's Peanut Brittle

Preparation Time: 30 minutes

Equipment: *A 15 x 10-inch rimmed cookie sheet, lined with parchment paper with an inch overhang on two of the sides, a digital read thermometer.*

This is not a conventional peanut brittle having more of a toffee crunch texture. My fondness for this peanut brittle began years ago when one of my friends gave it away at a neighborhood women's coffee group. We all loved it! The recipe was quickly exchanged amongst us. Many of us from the old neighborhood have kept in touch and some of us still go to a monthly book club. It has become a tradition for one of my friends, Sheila, to make this peanut brittle for our annual book club cookie exchange and, while not actually a cookie, we all clamor for our share of it. You will need a digital read thermometer for this recipe.

1½ cups peanut butter Chipits

1½ cups salted skinned cocktail peanuts

1½ cups salted butter

1¾ cups sugar

3 tablespoons light corn syrup

3 tablespoons water

1½ cups dark 54% Callebaut callets or Chipits for topping the brittle

Scatter the peanuts and peanut butter Chipits evenly over the prepared cookie sheet. Set aside.

In a medium to large heavy bottomed saucepan, melt the butter and add the sugar, corn syrup and water. Over medium high heat, stir the mixture and bring it to a boil. Allow the mixture to boil quite vigorously for two minutes before turning down the heat to medium low. Stirring all the while, continue to cook the syrup for approximately 20 minutes. Do not rush this process as the syrup at the bottom of the pan can burn easily. Over time the syrup will thicken and become a rich tawny brown color. It is ready when a digital read thermometer reads 310°F or 154°C. This is the hard crack stage. When the syrup reaches this temperature, carefully pour it over the peanuts and Chipits on your baking sheet. The syrup will spread naturally but you can help it with an offset spatula.

Wait five minutes, then scatter the chocolate callets or Chipits over the hardened but warm brittle. When the chocolate starts to melt, use an offset spatula or fork to spread the chocolate evenly over the brittle. Allow the brittle to cool at room temperature for at least 4 hours. When the chocolate has set you can refrigerate the pan of brittle for another 4 hours or overnight before breaking it up into pieces.

This brittle will keep in an airtight container in the refrigerator or cupboard for 3 weeks and can be frozen for up to 3 months.

Simple Accompaniments to Make your Desserts Pop

Fruits Marinated in Liqueurs

This is one of the easiest ways to add color, heighten flavor and add zing to almost any dessert. You can use a raspberry Chambord liqueur or a blackcurrant Cassis liqueur interchangeably with all kinds of berries.

RASPBERRIES & STRAWBERRIES IN CHAMBORD

Add to cakes, custards, pies, sweet biscuits, ice creams and sorbets. Particularly complements the flavors of lemon, almond, vanilla, and chocolate.

Marinate 1½ cups of raspberries/strawberries in 1 tablespoon sugar, 1 tablespoon of Chambord and 1 teaspoon of lemon juice.

BLACKBERRIES/BLACKCURRANTS/BLUEBERRIES IN CASSIS

Add to cakes, custards, pies, sweet biscuits, ice creams and sorbets. Particularly complements the flavors of lemon, vanilla, caramel, almond, hazelnut, and chocolate.

Marinate 1½ cups of blackberries/blackcurrants/blueberries in 1 tablespoon sugar, 1 tablespoon of Cassis and 1 teaspoon of lemon.

Peaches in Sauterne

Add to cakes, sweet biscuits, custards, ice creams and sorbets. Particularly complements the flavors of vanilla, caramel, blackberry/blackcurrant, pecan, and hazelnut.

Note: Marinate 6 peaches, thinly sliced in 1 cup sauterne and 4 tablespoon of honey. Recipe can be halved.

Almond Praline in Dark or Milk Chocolate

Add to tarts, pies, cakes, ice creams, sorbets, and mousses. Complements most flavors and adds a nice visual interest, height, and crunch to desserts.

Place 1 cup of sugar in a small heavy bottomed saucepan. Carefully add ¼ cup of water to the saucepan, pouring evenly over the sugar, being careful not to splash the sides of the pan. Bring the syrup to a boil and continue boiling, stirring only occasionally until the syrup reaches a rich amber color. Remove from the heat and add 1 tablespoon of butter. Stir to combine. Add ¾ cup of toasted chopped almonds and a pinch of salt. Stir to coat the almonds and then pour the almond brittle out on a parchment lined baking sheet. While still very warm to the touch, scatter ¾ cup dark or milk chocolate Callebaut callets or Chipits over the brittle. Spread evenly over the brittle with the tines of a fork or an offset spatula. When the chocolate is set, break into pieces.

Citrus Slices in Syrup
(can use oranges, lemons or limes)

Add to tarts, cakes, pastries, puddings, and mousses. Particularly complements the flavors of lemon, lime, orange, vanilla, and chocolate.

Bring ½ cup water and 1 cup sugar to a simmer in a small saucepan. Add thin slices of orange, lime, or lemon to the syrup. If using an orange, you can cut the slices in half. Simmer for 7 minutes, until the fruit is translucent but still holds together. Remove with a slotted spoon or spatula to a parchment lined baking sheet to cool. Continue simmering the syrup for 5 more minutes or until thickened. Remove the syrup from the heat, allow to cool, then brush over the fruit slices.

Revved Up Caramel Sauce
with Whiskey, Brandy or Rum

Add to ice creams, sorbets, bread puddings, cakes, tarts and custards. Particularly complements the flavors of vanilla, banana, apple, chocolate, blackberry, ginger and pumpkin.

Place 1 cup of sugar into a medium saucepan. Carefully add ¼ cup of water, being careful not to splash the sides. Over medium high heat, bring the syrup to a boil, whisking only occasionally. When the syrup turns a rich amber brown color, remove from the heat and add ¾ cup cream, 2 tablespoons salted butter and 2 tablespoons of alcohol of your choice. Return to the heat and allow the sauce to boil for 1 more minute, whisking constantly until the sauce is smooth. For less boil up when adding the cream, you can warm up the cream in the microwave for 40 seconds. Note: This sauce is wonderful plain, without any alcohol at all.

Raspberry Coulis or Sauce

Add to cakes, frostings, cheesecakes, tarts, custards, panna cottas, ice creams and sorbets. Particularly complements the flavors of chocolate, vanilla, and lemon.

In a small saucepan, heat ½ cup of good seedless raspberry jam, 1½ cups of fresh raspberries, ½ cup of sugar, 1 teaspoon of lemon juice and 1 tablespoon of Chambord (optional.) Bring the jam to a low boil for 5 minutes, stirring the jam occasionally to break up the fresh raspberries. Strain the jam into a heat proof bowl. Place the sieved jam back into the saucepan and bring to a boil, once more. Allow the sauce to boil for 7 minutes, until slightly reduced and thickened, then remove from the heat. Pour into a heat proof container and place, uncovered, in the refrigerator or freezer to cool.

Chocolate Sauce

Add to cakes, cheesecakes, ice creams, pastries, mousses, and sorbets. Particularly complements the flavors of hazelnut, pecan, vanilla, raspberry, blackberry, and chocolate.

In a heat proof bowl, add 1½ cup chopped 70% chocolate, or 54% Callebaut callets or Chipits, 1 tablespoon of butter and 1 tablespoon of corn syrup. Bring 1 cup of whipping cream to a simmer, just under a boil, in a medium sized saucepan. Pour the hot cream over the chocolate, wait 30 seconds and stir until smooth. Allow it to cool to lukewarm. If not using right away, refrigerate. Thin with 1 tablespoon of warmed whipping cream when ready to use.

Cheat Creme Fraiche

Add to tarts, fruit desserts, cakes, and pastries. Particularly complements rich desserts and the flavors of lemon, chocolate, ginger, nut and berry flavors.

Combine 1 tablespoon of sugar with 1 cup of regular fat sour cream and give it a good stir.

About the Author

GAIL SWEENEY has been baking and tweaking her recipes for over 25 years, providing specialty markets, bistros and boutique stores with her renowned goods. However, one of Gail's greatest pleasures is sharing her baking with her colleagues, neighbors, family and friends. "It always amazes me how the simple act of arriving with a plate of fresh baked cookies can change the atmosphere in a room, just by bringing people together to share some moments of happiness." From caramel banana cakes to chocolate praline tarts, all of Gail's bakes can be easily made ahead and frozen for those special moments.

When Gail is not baking, she works as a Child and Adolescent Psychologist, dividing her time between Toronto and Barrie, Ontario. She has three daughters and one young grandson Elliot, who shares her passion for all things sweet.

Recipe Index

A

15 Layer Crepe Cake with Hazelnut (Nutella) Chocolate Ganache 158
A Lemon Tart Worth Sharing 164
Alfajores with Dulce de Leche 54
Almond Cherry Rectangles in White Chocolate 33
Almond Praline in Dark or Milk Chocolate 248
Anzac Cookies for the 20 'Ohs 4
Apple Galette 175
Armagnac Date Squares 87

B

Banana Cake with Cream Cheese Icing, Caramel Drizzle & Maple Pecans 100
Billionaire Bars 89
Blood Orange Almond Tea Cake 103
Bourbon Butter Tarts 176
Brown Butter Caramel Cookies 18
Burnt Basque Cheesecake Topped with Pineapple Flowers 140
Butterscotch Crunch Cookies 73

C

Celestial Frozen Lemon Mousse Charlotte 232
Cheat Creme Fraiche 253
Cheesecake Brownies 82
Cherries Jubilee 228
Cherry Almond Oat Rounds in White Chocolate 27
Cherry Frangipane Tarts with Blackcurrant Jam 180
Cherry Pound Cake Loaf 132
Chocolate Crinkle Cookies with Caramel Cream 60
Chocolate Dipped Palmiers or Elephant Ears 66
Chocolate Ganache Cake 114
Chocolate Orange Butter Cookies 74
Chocolate Peanut Butter Cake with Chocolate Peanut Butter Icing 120
Chocolate Sauce 252

Citrus Slices in Syrup 249
Coconut Cream Cake with Chocolate Ganache 145
Coconut Cream Pie 199

D

Date & Nut Loaf 134
Date Night Chocolate Praline Tart 168
Decadent Dark Chocolate Cheesecake with Chocolate Ganache 142

E

Earthen Chocolate Cake 148
Easy Chocolate Lava Cakes 151
Empty Drawer Cookies 12
Engaging Lemon Layer Cake with Lemon Curd Filling 116
Espresso Brown Butter Blondies 84

F

Frozen Dulce de Leche Pie with Chocolate Crumb Crust 196
Fruit Marinated in Liqueurs 246

G

Ginger Crinkle Cookies 15
Gingerbread Dancers with White Chocolate 48
Goat Cheese Honey Roasted Fig Tart 208

H

Halva Brownies with Tahini Chocolate Drizzle 80
Hazelnut Linzer Cookies with Raspberry Jam 63
Holiday Thumbprint Cookies 36

I

Irish Whiskey Brioche Pudding with Whiskey Caramel Sauce 234

J

Jam Jar Cookies 70

L

Layered Chocolate Almond Oatmeal Bars 97
Lemon Explosion Cookies 68
Light as Air Angel Food Cake 155
Luscious Lemon Bars with Blackcurrant
    Jam 92

M

Mango Chocolate Tarts 189
Mango Cakelets on Fire 152
Maple Leaf Cookies with Maple Syrup
    Glaze 46
Maple Syrup Pecan Pie 191
Mile High Apple Filo Pie 171
Mille Feuille or Neopleon's 216
Mirror Glazed Chocolate Cake 112

N

Nana's British Berry Trifle 223
No Bake Cranberry Almond Date Bars 94
"Not Just a Cookie" Chocolate Dipped Espresso
    Hearts 30

O

Oatmeal Raisin Coconut Chocolate Chip
    Cookies 10
Old Fashioned Biscuit Shortcakes with Peaches
    in Sauterne 138
Old Fashioned Sour Cream Donut Cake 122
One Bowl Decadent Chocolate Cake
    Done 3 Ways 108
  Version 1: Raspberry Chocolate Cake with
      Chocolate Buttercream 110
  Version 2: Mirror Glazed Chocolate
      Cake 112
  Version 3: Chocolate Ganache Cake 114
Overnight Rich & Gooey Chocolate Chip
    Cookies 6

P

Peaches in Sauterne 247
Peanut Butter Cream Sandwich Cookies 50
Pear Tarte Tatin 215
Pecan Snowball Cookies 17
Persian Shortbread Cookies with Pistachios 44
Portuguese Custard Tarts 182
Profiteroles with Vanilla Pastry Cream &
    Chocolate Sauce 211

Pumpkin Loaf with Maple Glaze & Maple
    Pecans 136
Pumpkin Tarts with Sour Cream Glaze 185

R

Raspberry Chocolate Cake with Chocolate
    Buttercream 110
Raspberry Coulis or Sauce 251
Revved Up Caramel Sauce 250
Roasted Rhubarb & Strawberry Tray Bake 203
Ruby's Flourless Florentines 22

S

S'more Cookies 20
Salted Caramels Dipped in Chocolate 240
Scottish Shortbread Triangles 38
Sheila's Peanut Brittle 242
Shortbread Clouds 76
Shortbread Rounds with Vanilla Buttercream
    Icing 42
Simple Carrot Cake Made Glorious 126
Squareos with Mascarpone Cream Cheese
    Filling 52
Summer Peach & Blueberry Galette 206

T

Tipsy Tiramisu 230
Toffee Pecan Crunch 239
Triple Chocolate Shortbread 40
Tropical Key Lime Tart with Pistachio Graham
    Cracker Crust 194

V

Vanilla Bean Shorties with Raspberry
    Buttercream 58
Vanilla Cupcakes with Raspberry
    Buttercream 124
Vanilla, Vanilla Cake 129
Versatile & Delicious Sugar Cookies 24
Vintage Baked Alaska 225

W

White Chocolate Pecan Cookies 9
White Chocolate Strawberry Celebration
    Cake 236
Wild Blueberry Jelly Roll 105